3

Jean Lambert

1959

EDWARDIAN DAUGHTER

MYSELF
by Cecil Beaton

EDWARDIAN
DAUGHTER

BY

SONIA KEPPEL

HAMISH HAMILTON
LONDON

First published in Great Britain, 1958
by Hamish Hamilton Ltd
90 Great Russell Street London W.C.1
Copyright © 1958 by Sonia Keppel

PRINTED IN GREAT BRITAIN BY
EBENEZER BAYLIS AND SON, LIMITED, THE
TRINITY PRESS, WORCESTER, AND LONDON

TO

MY DARLING DAUGHTER

ROSALIND SHAND

FOREWORD

IN this attempted chronicle of the first twenty years of my life, having no diaries, I have picked out incidents important only to me, as I viewed them at the time. But for certain details concerning the '14–'18 war I am especially indebted to Major-General Sir Richard Howard-Vyse; Lord Gage; Colonel Dallas Waters; my cousins, Elizabeth Matheson and Rupert Keppel; and for a list of popular plays and songs of the period to Sir Norman Gwatkin and Mr. Michael Hornby. My family history would have been very incomplete without the knowledge and unstinted help of my aunt, Lady Cork, and my cousin, Lord Albemarle. To all these kind friends I offer my sincerest thanks, as also to Mrs. Lyons.

SONIA CUBITT

Hall Place
  West Meon
    Hants.
March 1958

CONTENTS

PART ONE

No. 30

I	THE WORLD INSIDE	3
II	GOING OUT	19
III	HOLIDAY VARIETY	32

PART TWO

No Fixed Address

IV	FELLOW TRAVELLERS	57
V	ENGLAND ÜBER ALLES	65
VI	MOUNTAIN SCENERY	76

PART THREE

No. 16

VII	SOCIAL OBLIGATIONS	83
VIII	END OF THE BANQUET	92

PART FOUR

Unknown Destinations

IX	MARCHING OFF TO WAR	107
X	1915	113

XI   1916   132

XII   1917   146

XIII   MARCHING TO A STANDSTILL   155

PART FIVE

The Final Move

XIV   KALEIDOSCOPIC LENS   169

XV   FAMILY INTRODUCTIONS   181

XVI   HOTEL ACCOMMODATION   190

XVII   LOHENGRIN AND ELSA   198

ILLUSTRATIONS

MYSELF, BY CECIL BEATON   *frontispiece*

PAPA INTRODUCING MAMMA TO
   HIS FAMILY, 1891   *facing page* 36

MAMMA AGED 18   37

MYSELF AS GREAT-UNCLE HARRY KEPPEL, 1903   68

VIOLET IN FANCY DRESS, 1903   69

MAMMA, 1906   100

PAPA, 1906   101

MAMMA PAINTED BY FLAMINGUE, 1908   132

MYSELF BEFORE THE 'UNVEILING'   133

EDWARD, 1917   164

ROLIE, 1918   164

SAN MORITZ, 1920   165

PART ONE

No. 30

Chapter One

THE WORLD INSIDE

MAMMA USED to tell me that she celebrated the Relief of Mafeking sitting astride a lion in Trafalgar Square. And that I was born a fortnight later.

I never doubted her story. From my earliest childhood she was invested for me with a brilliant, goddess-like quality, which made possible anything that she chose to say or do.

It seemed quite right that she should bestride a lion. Europa bestrode a bull, but the large, blonde Europa of my mythological picture-books in no way resembled my mother. In my extreme youth she drove a tandem of mettlesome ponies in a dog-cart. Had she decided to emulate Europa and ride a bull, she would not have let it take charge of her; she would have controlled it; and competently too; on a side-saddle. But somehow a bull was too plebeian a charger for my mother; a lion seemed much more fitting.

And fitting too was the fact of my easy birth so soon after Mafeking Night. Sometimes goddesses had difficult conceptions, but always they had safe deliveries. Possibly, I invested my birth with some Olympian quality too. But, if so, its goddess-like quality stopped with Mamma. Even she was powerless to transmit it to her daughters.

Despite her glorious health, on the day of my birth, Papa, and other anxious friends, smothered the road outside our house with straw, whereby to deaden the sound of traffic. For this was an age of chivalry, of putting women on pedestals. Mamma was adored in the Edwardian circle in which she moved, and, had she so wished, I feel sure that she could have decreed that her particular pedestal should have been made by Fabergé.

I can picture her as she lay back among her lace pillows, her beautiful chestnut hair, unbound around her shoulders, her alabaster skin, her turquoise-coloured eyes. She had all the qualities and none of the defects of an Alma Tadema beauty.

And I can see the flowers sent as oblations to this goddess, the orchids, the malmaisons, the lilies. Great beribboned baskets of them, delivered in horse-drawn vans by a coachman and attendant in livery. They would have been banked in tall, cut-glass vases about her bed. And she would have glowed in the midst of them easily absorbing into herself their colour, their scent and their sheen.

The fly in the ointment was myself, a scarlet-faced baby with (as my sister, Violet, candidly told me) 'a revoltingly bald head covered with strawberry jam'. Most unpleasantly, I believe, I was born with eczema. But it was yet another attribute of my mother's goddess-like qualities that she did not abhor the child she had borne. On the contrary, she appeared delighted with it; and so did my father. Only my sister resented its advent, and I think that was largely because it was so plain.

At their wedding the combined beauty of my father and mother had been sensational. In an age of giants he stood six feet four inches high, and in his Gordon Highlander bonnet, at nearly eight feet. Like her, he had eyes of bright blue. But whereas she had chestnut hair, his was black. And his magnificent breadth was a foil to her slender figure.

This Olympian couple first produced a pretty little daughter, curly-headed, dimpled and plump, obviously with looks that dressed up well as early photographs portrayed. This engaging child was a credit at parties and the pride of her parents and nurse. She seemed to cement the beauty of her parents; and for six unquestioning years she held it together.

Then I arrived.

And in that family of beautiful faces the first sight of my jam-covered head must have been as unpleasantly incongruous as a dwarf at a Veronese banquet. I must have cracked right across the looking-glass that Venus held up each morning. Except for the onslaughts on my life made by my sister, blissfully I was unconscious of it. But it must have been very apparent to other people.

Valiantly the routine tributes to beauty were continued. Where Violet had been photographed at six months, so was I: where she had been decked out in lace and ribbons, so was I: where, at six o'clock each evening, she was dressed up and brought down to the drawing-room, there to be admired by Mamma's friends and to be fed with cream on lumps of sugar, so was I. With unswerving loyalty, the same tributes to beauty were paid to me too. But the object of the tributes had changed value.

At six months both Violet and myself were photographed naked and, probably for prudent reasons, sitting on straw. She had a faint down on her head; I was hairless. It must be admitted that at that age she was merely clearing the decks for beauty. She still had quite a way to go. But, by the next photograph, she was established. Whereas each succeeding photograph of myself developed me plainer and plainer.

I ruined the tradition of Violet's placid 'staying-put', too. Within five minutes of being decked out in them, my lace and ribbons were bedraggled and torn. And, downstairs in the drawing-room, first I greedily absorbed the lumps of sugar and then, as greedily, made tracks for my next delectable course, in the coal-scuttle.

Such trivial discrepancies in the beautiful picture did not disturb my mother. Unique among goddesses, she had a sense of humour. Possibly for her, my ludicrous inclusion in its framework even enhanced its value. For the Veronese dwarf could be jester as well. Whatever the reason, she made me feel part of it and, except for Violet's guided missiles, in it I felt secure.

The house wherein I was born was on the west side of Portman Square.

The square was elegantly constructed, mainly of eighteenth century houses to which had been added a few concessions to modern comfort inside. (I think we had electric light: and Mamma and Papa had two bathrooms leading out of each other.) But such concessions were few. Refrigerators were unknown, and the food was kept cool outside the house in an area larder. Regularly, the housemaid developed 'housemaid's knee' on her knees, dusting. There was no telephone, and no central heating. And two bathrooms probably were considered extravagant luxuries by many of the other inmates of the square.

Like a protecting family umbrella, Queen Victoria still hovered over her subjects. But she was getting very light, poor old lady, and a mere puff of wind might soon blow her away. Outside the periphery of the umbrella the sky was clearing fast. From decorous grey it was becoming rather a blatant blue. As yet there were patches only of this blue sky, and no one dared leave the umbrella's protection for long. But the sun of a new era was beginning to break through, and soon the umbrella would be exchanged for parasols of a lighter structure.

In this new sunshine did the metamorphosis of taste take place overnight, I wonder? Were the auction rooms cluttered up suddenly with ottomans and discarded antimacassars? If so, somebody bought them, for they have all come back again. But in London, in the newly gay houses to which my parents took me, the solid Maple's furniture, the Turkey pile, the dismal reps, were nearly all eliminated in the first years of King Edward VII's reign.

Admittedly, something much less lasting replaced them. Taste took a feminine, frivolous turn, expressing itself in little gilt 'papiermâché' chairs, in 'chaises-longue', smothered with lace cushions, in 'Lady Teazle' screens, covered with machine-made Beauvais, in masses of maddeningly midget tables. The colours became nebulous. As a transition between grey and blue, mauve predominated. The new sunshine was shut out at an early hour each day, and artificially replaced with light glowing softly through pink shades. The character (and cost) of the flower-decoration changed completely. Orchids replaced begonias; malmaisons replaced petunias. I may be anticipating this floral change by a year or two, and the orchids and mal-maisons may have been still in bud in 1900. But, whereas in Queen Victoria's reign 'paterfamilias' predominated and male taste prevailed, now, in King Edward VII's reign, the deifica-tion of the feminine was re-established.

In my family such deification was inevitable. But more than one goddess made up my mother in whom, unexpectedly, Minerva took precedence of Venus. So the femininity in her drawing-room was less challenging and more conciliatory than in many. Solidly comfortable chairs had their place there; and the curtains were not drawn till the daylight faded.

Shortly before I was born, my parents had moved to Port-man Square from Wilton Crescent. The house in Wilton Crescent I never knew, but the house in Portman Square must have been a prelude in taste to the one they had later. Accord-ing to contemporary standards, I am sure it was pretty. But, at the time of my birth, some of the ingredients of Mamma's later taste must have been lacking.

One necessary ingredient was money which, at this time, neither my mother nor father possessed in great measure. He had been one of ten, and she one of nine, children, and, at the time of their marriage, beauty and charm had been their main dowry. It opened doors to them wherever they went and, by the time I was born, some of the doors had led to good business. But the financial security behind the doors had not yet been established.

No. 30 Portman Square was narrow and high, each floor of which acquired significance for me as I grew older. The base-ment spelt breath-taking adventure and, as yet, unknown risk. The ground floor was largely a changing-room (shawls on, to go out; shawls off, to come in). The drawing-room floor was

given over to fun. My day-nursery floor was a white-painted
fortress, my nurse the garrison-commander; my sister's French
governess, a spirited captain of the guard. The attic (and night-
nursery) floor smelt of Brasso, and perspiration, and soap.
And different sounds went with the floors: sepulchral voices
and the clatter of mysterious vessels in the basement; muted
sounds of perambulator wheels in the hall; enchanted laughter,
male and female, in the drawing-room; altercations in North-
country English and shrill French on the nursery ramparts,
accompanied by a rattle as of artillery, from an adjacent pipe;
sniffs and the rustle of starchy petticoats came from the attic.
The house became my orchestra, and quickly I learned the
score it followed.

In the course of the day the position of the floors was
reversed. I started at the top and worked my way down. First,
I had an uncomfortable sojourn in a hip-bath in the night-
nursery, with my behind very hot, and my back very cold.
Then suffocating layers of merino underclothes were piled on
me, topped by a pinafore. Thereafter, I scrambled down the
top flight of stairs to breakfast in the day-nursery. (For me,
'night' and 'day' nursery had literal interpretations. The attic
roof of the 'night'-nursery precluded all human contact and all
but a small patch of sky from my sight. The 'day'-nursery
looked out on to the world, and the light, and the people.)
After breakfast followed an unendingly delightful visit to
Mamma, in bed, and Papa, breakfasting in his room next door.
A brief reversal to the night-nursery before going out. Then a
syncopated progress down the main flight of stairs to the hall.
And so out. And so in.

At first, the fortress floor controlled all my movements, and
any expedition outside it was tacitly on parole.

In her creaseless white apron and high starched collar, my
garrison-commander was as imposing a figure as a general in
the tropics. She controlled all the incomings and outgoings of
the garrison, including those (under protest) of the captain of
the guard. As her lieutenant, her nursery-maid carried out the

day's orders and, as her ensign, Violet stood to attention when she passed.

Occasionally, there were inspections from visiting generals, which entailed an unwelcome period of 'spit-and-polish' first. Although carried out in a friendly manner, these inspections were formal. There were hawk-eyed appraisals of the garrison-quarters; and apparently cursory (but alertly fault-finding) appraisals of the garrison-kit. The visiting general would be accompanied by one or two reluctant recruits like myself. These were detailed to play with me in the middle of the guard-room while the two generals retired to a far corner to converse. On such occasions, my garrison-commander could not count on much support from her captain. (Recruited from the Foreign Legion, she deployed military tactics of her own.) But her lieutenant's smart bearing usually came in for praise.

Sometimes (and far more excitingly), there were skirmishes with enemy forces. The boot-boy was an adept at commando attack; and it had to be admitted that, on occasions, the authority of the commander was positively challenged by the captain. But the skirmishes had only the strength of harrying forces, and to all their attacks the commander apparently, presented an inviolable front.

Yet, once outside the fortress floor, she had to acknowledge others of superior station. Mr. Rolfe, the butler, and Mrs. Wright, the cook, accorded her full military honours, but they did so with royal condescension. As Pluto and Proserpine they held kingly rank.

Surprisingly, under her martial exterior, Nannie had a snail's soft body. In the early morning light, under her voluminous nightgown, I could descry the pink folds of it. Then, as she got up and dressed, it fascinated me to see how she tucked them back under control. At one moment I could see the outline of a huge shoulder above the bath; then, its eclipse behind a bath-towel; then, its emergence again for a tantalizing minute, as she put on her bodice and stertorously pulled up her stays. (Both these processes appeared to be simultaneous, as though they were assisted by an invisible pair of hands.) There followed the camouflage of her petticoat, concealing the pulling on of knickers; more whalebone, more starch, clamping down a vast bosom; the fastening of sharp buckles and a brooch, like the riveting of armour. With each controlling layer the pink folds were packed back into their shell until only I, as an eye-witness, knew of the vulnerability beneath her crustaceous façade.

On their 'off-duty' Nannie's subordinates were treated with strict justice and, during these periods, her barriers were down. During playtime, many a doll's tea-party did I set out on the military escarpments of her enormous chest when, to liven up proceedings (and threatening the tea-party like thunder), Nannie would sing.

Her song (always fragments of the same one) was incomprehensible:

'Lady Wondser lived a maiden,
Pure and bright, and liketty fur.' Or
'She was but a village-painter
And a landscape-maiden, he.'

The sense did not matter. What counted, in frivolous, precious moments, was the sound.

Playtime for me started early, playing horses on Nannie's bed, from which point of vantage I had an oblique view of her dressing.

This led to my first accident. At the age of two, I fell off her bed behind the po-stand, and broke my collar-bone.

Into this first accident a psychiatrist read a lot. He said the shock of it first produced in me a nervous asthma which has dogged much of my life ever since. As a reaction to fright, also he said that it affected me subconsciously so that, whenever danger or anxiety threatened me thereafter, I got it again. And, as my first clear memory of childhood, he said that it was important in shaping my character. Such were his premises. Who is to prove that they were right?

Certainly I remember the accident as painful and frightening; and certainly the shock of it took away my breath.

But its sequel was completely satisfying.

To set my collar-bone, Mamma took me to a doctor and, because he was rough setting it, she boxed his ears.

From that moment for me she became a goddess, as even Jupiter's lightning could not have produced greater consternation than this action of hers.

The world of Pluto and Proserpine continued unexplored. Sometimes the door to it was left open and, fascinated, I peered down. Above ground I knew and loved both Mr. Rolfe and Mrs. Wright. Both were corpulent, smiling figures, given to kind teasing and fat laughter. But in their nether, unknown kingdom they acquired for me satanic status, presiding over fearful rites.

The stairs to their region were steep and very narrow, covered with slippery linoleum. On them, feet had an animal, stampeding sound, like cloven hoofs careering down a mountainside. At the end of each journey the footsteps died away in silence. What, I wondered, paved this pit?

In my house orchestra, sounds and time became synonymous. From dawn to dark I knew what time each sound portended, from Nannie's waking grunt at seven each morning to her benedictory peck at seven each night. Thereafter, tacitly, she expected me to sleep, but sometimes I slept badly, and then the timepiece of my night extended further. Sounds of Nannie's supper below me at seven-thirty; the banging of Violet's door at nine; the final poking out of the day-nursery fire at nine-thirty; the clicking shut of the nursery gate within five minutes; Nannie's ponderous climbing up the stairs at twenty minutes to ten. Thereafter, her one-minute progress between the top of the stairs and the door of the night-nursery gave me time to pretend to be asleep.

Between eight and nine at night, all doors seemed shut, with people oblivious of me on the other side. During that hour the dial of sound showed blank, waiting for me to fill it in.

One night I heard Nannie's lieutenant take in the nursery supper. I allowed time for her and Nannie to start their ruminative chewing. (Why was it that nursery-maids seemed to suck, not bite, all food?) And then I rose.

In my nightgown and on naked feet, I crept towards and opened, the night-nursery door. The house was quiet. Rounding the bend of the staircase, I reached the fortress floor. At night, often I had wondered what happened on it behind closed doors. Now I listened. But only a murmur of voices came to my ears, suddenly punctuated by shrill laughter from the guard-room.

I came to the nursery gate. So far, alone, I had never been outside it. I slid my finger into the latch, opened it and was in the world outside. Fearfully I paused. Surely someone would cry: 'Prisoner escaped!' But all stayed quiet. I ventured on.

Each floor went slowly past me, muffled and strange; and very frightening. Witches and bats came out at night and, in this alien world, I might be attacked from any side. Almost in tears, and clutching the banisters, I stumbled on.

One terrifying factor: the skylight had gone. During the day, the light came gaily through it. Now it had vanished. And, instead, a black pall hung over the main staircase, like a lid clamped down.

More and more fearfully I descended, longing for one of the strange, tall doors to open to emit someone I knew. But still they held themselves aloof. Then, at last, I came down into the front hall, where pile carpet gave way suddenly to cold marble under my bare feet.

One half of the front hall had borrowed light from a street lamp; the other was dark. And at the other end of the darkness was the basement door.

I peered into the darkness. It seemed as thick as a curtain.

Would it smother me with its sable folds? Or, if I jumped into it fast enough, would it give way to let me through? My adventure was becoming a nightmare. The darkness began to move.

Terrified, I looked back up the staircase to the dim, gaunt doors. No friend to help me there. Each hostile sentinel would confront me again. I dared not face them. Once I got through the black curtain, as an important hostage (my parents' daughter) there was a chance that Pluto and Proserpine might treat me well. The risk was tremendous, but worth taking. And, anyway, I had no choice.

With a squeal like a small, frightened piglet, I rushed through the dark patch to the basement door (which was open).

My bare foot slipped on the slippery top step and I rolled over and over. Lights, cries of astonishment, a gathering crowd of people. Pluto's indignant voice: 'Really, what a time for Mrs. Eeles to send down the washing!' Then, as the washing uncurled itself: 'Lor', it's Miss Sonia!'

Sensually, I loved the smell of Mamma's room, with its flower smells, and a certain elusive smell, like fresh green sap, that came from herself. And the smell of Papa's room (hair oil and tobacco), next door. And I loved their thrilling intimacy, generously extended to me. At best, armed neutrality existed on the fortress floor. But on my parents' floor a different comradeship existed, a comradeship of love and laughter, without weapons. And this comradeship included me.

My visits followed a daily pattern.

Each morning I visited Mamma's room where, enchantedly, I played with all the lovely things she had worn the night before. (The cornucopia of Ceres, spilling out for me.) Then I migrated to Papa's room where, equally enchanted, I watched this benevolent giant eat a giant's meal. Two boiled eggs, two fried eggs, an omelette, and kidneys and bacon usually made up his breakfast. I was allowed to crack the eggs with a knife, and to spread his buttered toast with jam. Alertly, I stood at his side with his arm round me, and it never occurred to either of us that I should sit down. Thereafter, I was allowed to watch him shave, and to watch him curl his magnificent moustache with tiny tongs.

In the drawing-room, my evening ritual took place at six.

Thereafter, about half an hour later, I repaired to Papa's sitting-room, there to curl up on his knee and, with my head on his shirt-front, to listen to tales of adventure. Always he read me boys' books. Or he told me boys' stories. The world of women was left behind. Even Mamma could have no place in our crew of two. With his shirt-front as a trusty prow against sudden danger, nightly he and I set sail for the open sea.

Sometimes, my contacts with my parents took the form of dress displays. They would go out to special functions. Or they would give a dinner-party. At all times of day or year their clothes seemed beautiful. And those my father wore were as exciting as my mother's. In a front seat in their dress circle, I had a splendid view.

I can remember a spring dress of Mamma's, in a grey and white stripe. Below a boned, high collar, it cascaded in widening folds down her bosom to her slender waist. And from her throat to her knees, it was buttoned with tiny, braid buttons. To set it off, Papa wore a dark blue, skin-tight frock-coat, worn with a top hat. He wore this coat over his shirt and, when paying afternoon calls, he could not take it off. In his lapel he wore a carnation. In those days, if calling on a lady at tea time, implicitly he had to give the impression that he was merely 'looking in'. Into her drawing-room he carried all the paraphernalia of his walk: his top hat, his walking-stick, his gloves. And gentlemen callers on my mother did the same. And I can remember a black velvet, low-cut evening dress of Mamma's, with which she wore a huge, black, feathered hat. With it, as jewellery, she wore a high diamond and pearl dog-collar, pearl ear-rings, and a diamond drop. In those days, the contours of Ceres were more fashionable than those of Venus, and my mother's ripe curves were much admired. To conform to such standards, handkerchiefs padded out some of the bodices of her flatter-chested friends. As a partner in her magnificence, Papa wore a gardenia, and a coat with satin facings and a very tall top hat. Small wonder that, in my front seat in their dress circle, I sat there, open-mouthed.

But these were special occasions, excluding intimacy. Best, I love to think of Mamma, in her frilly petticoat and lace dressing-jacket, brushing her hair. And of Papa, in his green velvet smoking-suit, bending over my bed to say 'good night'.

Pluto and Proserpine vanished from their kingdom, and now I was accorded liaison duties between Nannie and the basement.

Gone were my fears of Mr. Rolfe and Mrs. Wright, and of their black, satanic pit. On inspection, I found it paved with cork lino, silent to walk on, and containing a bright kitchen with shiny pans, and tins of spices and cake, and sugar.

My liaison duties followed Mrs. Wright's morning visit to my mother, to whom each day she brought a black, shiny book of the day's menus for her to accept or veto. This book Mamma would consider carefully, scratching out, writing in. And while she did so Mrs. Wright would stand motionless, except for a brooch of cornelian which jumped convulsively beneath her high net collar. After her visit, now I carried her book down for her to the kitchen, and received in exchange a small packet of tea or sugar to take back to the nursery store-cupboard. And, very often, Mr. Rolfe gave me some token of his trust as well. I was tremendously proud of my duties in the basement, which gave me a drummer-boy status on the fortress floor.

Mrs. Wright had a devoted slave who had proudly respon-sible moments once weekly, when Mrs. Wright went out. She it was who cooked the schoolroom and nursery meals; and who carried the plates from the kitchen to 'The Hall'.

Mr. Rolfe, Mrs. Wright, Miss Draper, Katie, Peggie and George all lived together in 'The Hall', which, at first, sounded draughty but which, on inspection, seemed just an ordinary, warm, comfortable room.

Mr. Rolfe slept in the basement as did also his slave, George, the boot-boy. Both their rooms had much the status of dungeons, brightened up with Turkey rugs. Through bars they looked out on to the area and never saw the sun.

Between the kitchen and Mr. Rolfe's bedroom was the back door. This led out to the area-steps which led up I knew not whither. The top of the door hid the world from my sight, but light came down the steps, and figures, starting with their feet. The shoeing of the feet varied with their trades, and gradually I knew each pair by sight. The huge, shapeless boots of the dustman and coalheaver resembled each other, but the dustman had tabs on his which the coalheaver had not. The milkman's boots were smaller and lighter. The boots of the postman turned up at the toes. Long before their shoulders and heads appeared I knew the identity of the backdoor-tradesmen by the soles of their feet. Especially, I was intrigued by the milkman's feet, whose appearance was presaged by a strange, echoing call and a far-away clatter of pony's hoofs.

During the time in which I visited the basement there was an interval when I was in 'no-man's-land'. This was in the passage, between the kitchen and the staircase back to the front hall. I was on lenient parole in this passage, which was considered devoid of adventure by everyone but myself.

One sunny morning, from the door of the kitchen I watched the postman arrive. As was his custom, he went into Mr. Rolfe's bedroom across the passage, there to deliver the letters and to have a little chat with his friend. Behind him the back door was open, and suddenly I was through it and up the area-steps.

Up till then I had known the world of people from a distance only, from the top of its head, or the soles of its feet. Then, suddenly, I was on its same foot-level, but rather low down, about up to its knees. At this level, its head was still far above me, like a Rackham drawing of a human face with the limbs of trees.

I seemed more in touch with the horse-drawn world. An omnibus, with a lidful of people; a smart private hansom, with its coachman perched high on its box; a dray drawn by two dappled horses with tails tied up with ribbons and with huge, feathered feet; and a water-cart, rattling slowly towards me with plumes of water spraying out behind it like a peacock's tail.

At the corner of the square, the cart stopped beside me, and I noticed that it had a ledge across the back of it and a step up beside the back wheel. No one seemed to notice me as I climbed up on to the water-cart. And thereafter, I was partially concealed behind a wall of spray.

We forged across Portman Square as though drawn by sea-horses. The traffic surged and ebbed round us with an ocean's swell. I felt rather sick but elated, and as wet as a mermaid. So I was sorry when the cart hove-to in Wigmore Street.

To my alarm, a policeman approached the back of it, and lifted me off it, and put me on my feet.

Once back on the pavement I was a prey to the world of people, and this time, inquisitively, the human face peered directly down at me through its limbs of trees. Gone was the security I had felt in mid-ocean. The sea-horse-drawn world was now quite out of reach. Like a fish out of water, I felt breathless and parched. A small, stateless mermaid, without name or address.

The policeman asked my name. I answered 'Baby'. My anonymity seemed permanent. The limbs of the people crowded round me like roots. Fortunately, he discovered a label to give me identity: a small gold bangle with a pendant diamond 'S'. Carefully he assessed it and my relative value to it. Then he carried it and me to the police-station in Marylebone Lane.

There, an hour later, Papa found me. By which time, cheerfully, I had adapted myself to my new life in prison. Around me the charge-room had acquired nursery status. On the centre table I sat wrapped in a blanket, while my pinafore hung to dry in front of the stove. My face and hands had been washed, and my hair had been brushed. From a mug one policeman was giving me sips of hot milk; another was spreading jam on bread for me. A third had lent me his policeman's whistle, which sound was piercingly clear, as Papa arrived. To me then, there seemed little to choose between prison and fortress, except policemen to play with and more bread and jam.

But my liaison duties were cut down on return to the fortress, and free patrols to the basement were brought to an end. And from then on my garrison-commander raised her voice more often: 'Please shut the nursery-gate. And keep Baby in.'

Chapter Two

GOING OUT

ACROSS THE square was No. 38, inhabited by Lord
and Lady Alington, my parents' great friends.
The frame of their house was the same shape as ours,
but it was larger and heavier. The background was more
sumptuous; the food was richer; and, inside the frame, the
principal figures weighed considerably more. In this house the
Veronese banquet continued without ceasing. Always the curtains seemed drawn. The flower-scents were stifling. Valhalla
supplanted Olympus. And Lady Alington herself seemed a
permanently recumbent Brünnhilde.

The component figures in the picture had been rearranged.
Voluptuously, Lady Alington filled the foreground. And,
instead of the dwarf-jester, now indulgently she played
with a pretty little (human) monkey and a lithe Nubian
slave.

To this overwhelming house Mamma used constantly to
take me, and still I can feel my sensation of dread as we reached
the front door. In a few more minutes I would be tormented
by the monkey. To all outward appearances the monkey
(Loïs) was charming. But she had sharp claws and teeth. With
sublime wishful thinking, our mutual parents proclaimed us
great friends. And our nurses seemed so friendly. The convenient proximity of our parents' houses overruled all doubts.

Everything at No. 38 seemed to happen near the front hall.
As we went in the hall seemed teeming with butlers and footmen; Lord Alington would often emerge from the dining-

room to greet my mother; and Gerard Sturt (the elder son) usually seemed to be going out. At the back of the hall was a tiny flower-room, with a pent-roof ceiling, under the stairs. In our house it contained Papa's holiday fishing tackle, the carriage umbrella and my mail-cart. It was Lady Alington's boudoir at No. 38.

Every hothouse flower imaginable was packed in around her 'chaise-longue'. Outsize orchids, outsize malmaisons, outsize lilies. They acted on me like an anaesthetic, and when I went in to thank Lady Alington for a tea-party, I saw her through half-closed eyes. But my vision of her remains unforgettable. Out of a billowing ocean of lace and ribbons, still I can see her pale face and full lips and small alert eyes. Somehow her eyes were at variance with the rest of her large, lazy body. The eyes of a squirrel in a magnolia tree. Squeezed in among the flowers and furniture was usually some gentleman. What with his top hat and gloves and walking-stick, he had hardly room to move.

In measure as we ascended to the nursery floor the air grew noticeably cooler. And often, on the nursery floor, it seemed positively cold. This illusion was created by the monkey's keeper, a small, malevolent personality aptly named Mrs. Whatmore.

Mrs. Whatmore adored her charges, Napier and Loïs, but she seemed to hate all other children. And she extended her hate to the children's nurses. Almost at once she sensed Nannie's vulnerability under her shell. She prodded it cleverly: 'Her Ladyship always insists on *real* lace on Loïs's underclothes.' 'Thank goodness! I don't have to curl up *Loïs's* hair in curl-papers at night.' Nannie would rumble like heavy artillery, but she was no match for Mrs. Whatmore in assault tactics.

The Nubian slave, Napier, and the monkey, Loïs, were as unlike Lady Alington's two elder children as north from south. Diana and Gerard were Scandinavian and shy; Napier and Loïs were Latin in manners and looks. In the family picture,

Diana and Gerard stayed aloof in the background. In the front, Napier and Loïs played merrily with their mother's rings.

Lord and Lady Alington entertained lavishly, yet the silence seemed permanent on the two upper floors. No doubt, at night these were lit up and festive. But in the daytime they seemed empty and aloof from every-day use.

The main social activity took place in or near Kundry's garden, and here everyone was expected to act with Wagnerian zeal. Although looking incongruous, in this milieu Napier and Loïs provided much-needed gaiety. Like a pair of tumblers, they took the eye off the backcloth between the scenes.

To my dismay, early I discovered that I was expected to be part of their comic turn. At home, with my own props, this would have been no great hardship to me. But, as a visiting jester, I lacked confidence, and quickly degenerated into an awkward little clown. For the first time I became self-conscious, a defect which was quickly exploited by the monkey and her keeper. The Nubian slave was much kinder, but already he was too much of an artist not to subordinate kindness to the success of his turn.

So, practically on every visit to the Alingtons' house, when they and their guests were present, I had to submit to a form of calf-baiting, accompanied by little gracefully administered nips and pinches which, while not violent enough to produce tears, yet left me feeling hurt and bewildered. Having no previous experience of them I had no idea how to parry them. My inability to do so provoked roars of applause from the audience, and gradually I learnt to disguise my discomfiture and to pretend that my clumsy clowning was deliberate. By so doing, now I like to think that I got a bit of my own back on the monkey and her keeper. At all events, I did not disgrace myself as the main comic element in the turn.

The thing that surprised me was that Mamma seemed unaware of the calf-baiting. With her powers of perception I felt that she should have realized my discomfiture at once. Perhaps, to her, lack of self-confidence was unthinkable. Or she felt that

I must learn to defend myself. Or perhaps she just saw the whole trivial scene in proportion. Whatever she saw or felt, she made no comment. And probably her silence was my moral help.

The Alington household was the hub of the big wheel of Edwardian fashion, setting in motion the gilded structure with its elegant concourse of people. Looking back now I feel that it may have possessed rather a pantomime quality. The hub of the wheel of Cinderella's coach drawn by high-stepping horses which, one day, might turn back into mice. But, at the time, it seemed splendid. And the wheel was lavishly painted and generously oiled for smooth running and pleasure.

To my child's eyes the glitter of the whole coach was blinding; and only occasionally was it that particular personages in it detached themselves from their scintillating fellows for my recognition.

King Edward himself, with his beard and kind, deep voice and plump, beringed hands and cigars; Prince Francis of Teck, beloved by all generations; my godmothers, Countess Torby and Mrs. Ronald Greville; Sir Ernest Cassel; Sir Thomas Lipton; Lady Sarah Wilson, whose courage during the siege of Ladysmith had made her a heroine.

As was to be expected, before confronting this formidable array of people, my garrison-commander drilled me for correct bearing: 'Always curtsy to the King, dear,' she would say.

I tried to carry out her orders but, in my new-found shyness, sometimes I made mistakes. I dared not look higher than beard-level so played safe and curtsied to the cigar and rings. Sir Ernest Cassel, too, had a beard and wore rings and smoked cigars; so, more often than not, he came in for the curtsy.

Back in my own home, these personages seemed much less frightening. And, indeed, on occasions they developed an unexpectedly nursery-quality more suited to the fortress than the drawing-room floor.

Sometimes, King Edward (Kingy) came to tea with

Mamma, and was there when I appeared at six o'clock. On such occasions he and I devised a fascinating game. With a fine disregard for the good condition of his trouser, he would lend me his leg, on which I used to start two bits of bread and butter (butter side down), side by side. Then, bets of a penny each were made (my bet provided by Mamma) and the winning piece of bread and butter depended, of course, on which was the more buttery. The excitement was intense while the contest was on. Sometimes he won, sometimes I did. Although the owner of a Derby winner, Kingy's enthusiasm seemed delightfully unaffected by the quality of his bets.

Both Countess Torby and her husband, the Grand Duke Michael, were my godparents, and to me, inevitably, they were associated with the exquisite Fabergé ornaments on my mother's table. I thought they made them. Even now I seem to see Countess Torby arriving with an enormous muff out of which, with an irresistibly infectious laugh, she would conjure me a present. And the Grand Duke Michael had a wonderful gold cigarette case of elaborate mechanism which lit and then snuffed itself with a silken cord passed through the back of it.

My other godmother, Mrs. Ronald Greville, resembled a small Chinese idol with eyes that blinked. She, too, gave me beautiful presents: jewellery, dolls, a dog. This last was a Japanese spaniel closely resembling herself. In the nick of time Mamma prevented my loyally calling it 'Maggie', and it was christened 'Yama'. It was a dull little dog, with an inferiority complex, and very different in character from her own Pekingese spaniels, which filled the void in her childless life and which she adored.

I did not overcome my awe of Sir Ernest Cassel and never attempted to submit his trousers to the buttery tests endured by King Edward's. But very often his beringed hands, too, extended me a present so that, although I never dared to play with him, I came to rely on him as a living form of gilt-edged security, a likeness which was enhanced by his wearing shirts with broad parallel stripes on them, like the bars in front of a cashier's desk.

Sir Thomas Lipton had a very different personality, genial and breezy; just the right sort to be at the head of his trading-fleet of tea-planters. Almost, I was prepared to include him with my father and myself in our crew. Even on the most formal occasions he had a salt tang about him, and never would I have been surprised if he had arrived to call with a parrot in a cage and a ring in one ear.

I put Lady Sarah Wilson in the same category as Miss Florence Nightingale whom sometimes I saw, from the windows of Dorchester House, being pushed in her bath-chair in the garden in South Street. Both ladies had been heroines and as such were awe-inspiring. But Miss Nightingale must have been one a long time before. Lady Sarah seemed cheerfully forgetful of her former heroism and content to let it lie, preserved in lavender, until the advent of another war. She, too, was kindly disposed to play games with me, which she did with military gusto as though she were on the recreation-ground at Camberley.

Mixed with Mamma's other guests were, of course, her relations. But between her and her sisters the disparity in age was so great that they seemed more like her aunts.

I cannot remember my maternal grandmother. My grandfather was born two years before Napoleon's retreat from Moscow and was much older than she was, and was nearly sixty when my mother was born. My grandmother had been brought up in Greece. Throughout her life apparently she preserved a fascinatingly nymph-like quality, rather oddly reproduced in some of her daughters.

Mamma's sisters were unevenly divided into two categories: those who ruled others and those who were overruled. Half-way down in age, but at the head of the troupe in forcefulness, was my Aunt Jessie who had much in common with my garrison-commander, except that Aunt Jessie's sense of nursery discipline was based on theory and not on experience. Then came my Aunts Louie, Sophy, Dolly and Frances, in increasing order of diffidence; obversely followed by Aunt May, high-spirited, determined and dashing.

Right down the list came my Uncle Archie and, eleven months later, my mother. A previous son had died in infancy and, after so many daughters, my uncle's advent had been treated with awe. Figuratively speaking, he was drawn up with tongs. Definitely, he was tabulated with his more timid sisters. But from the first, Mamma was ranged with her two forceful sisters where her superabundant vitality maintained the balance between ruler and ruled.

On my father's side, his mother, old Lady Albemarle, maintained her matriarchal position through unsleeping vigilance. To do so I suspect that sometimes she used her old age as a big stick with which to belabour her children. She, too, had more daughters than sons. Of those living remained Aunt Theo, Aunt Hilda, Aunt Lena, Aunt Susan, Aunt Mary and Aunt Florence. Her eldest son was Lord Albemarle; after him, Uncle Derek; and, lastly, Papa. Her daughters were all forceful and clear-cut, like black-and-white silhouettes. Where most of my mother's sisters were Dryads, my father's sisters were Amazons. And, given the opportunity, the Amazons would have made short work of the Dryads, as the Dryads very well knew.

With the exception of my father's sisters Hilda and Lena, at some time or other both Amazons and Dryads were married. Rumour had it that Aunt Jessie had led Uncle Ted by the collar, but most of her sisters' husbands seemed to boss their wives. Aunt Louie's husband was Major of the Tower of London, and, despite Mamma's assurance of his kindness and leniency, inwardly I was sure that frequently he consigned Aunt Louie to Guy Fawkes's minute torture-chamber, 'Little Ease'. Aunt May's husband, Uncle Graham, was a Lord Advocate of Scotland, and, though she appeared unabashed, probably he put her on secret trials at home. The rest of the Dryads' husbands I knew only as ether which, clearly, through constant administration, had 'softened-up' all resistance in their wives.

Some of my uncles and aunts lived in the country; some in London; some in both. In Mamma's family, those within reach met regularly on Sunday afternoons at Aunt Jessie's house in Wilton Street.

Aunt Jessie's house was small but with an infinite capacity for 'packing in'. On Sundays it was like a school trunk, bursting open to admit 'just one more thing'.

One exciting thing about it was the dangerous situation of the lavatory on the landing. If you opened its door without thinking, you fell down the stairs. Once Cousin Johnnie Pearith (a great faller) fell out of it; and it was whispered that once Aunt Jessie herself had done so. But she never admitted to this.

The drawing-room was crowded with furniture and knick-knacks, and once inside it, like furled umbrellas, Aunt Jessie's relations stood upright and motionless with their arms to their sides. Now and then, obeying her command, nervously one of them would extend an arm, and eagerly I would await the inevitable crash of china or furniture that followed the move-ment.

If Aunt Jessie wanted Sweeby, like a ship's captain on the bridge, she 'blew' for her on a tube. A minute or two would pass and then, purple of face, Sweeby would burst into the room as though obeying the imperative command: 'All hands on deck!'

The younger members of Aunt Jessie's tea-party were allowed to sit down, and, to their delight, their part of the tea-party was conducted in miniature—tiny cups and saucers and plates, tiny scones, tiny cakes; even the bread and butter was cut in midget slices. At this level the younger members were free to 'make a good tea', a treat which was denied to their grown-up constricted relations who were almost bound to refuse cup or bite.

Papa's family seemed more dispersed; or I saw it less often.

Grannie 'B.' lived in Lowndes Street; Uncle Arnold and Aunt Gertie in Belgrave Square; Aunt Lena in a convent at Roehampton; and Uncle Derek and Aunt Bridget lived close to Buckingham Palace because of his work. Of all these I preferred to visit Uncle Arnold and Aunt Gertie who usually had crumpets for tea.

At five years old, Mamma took me to my first play, admittedly a most unsuitable choice for one so young.

Clearly I remember that it was a matinée about Nero, fiddling madly before the burning of Rome. A deafening thunderstorm went on in the background, through which Agrippina shrieked valedictions to her insensitive son. Alternately, the stage glowed red from the flames consuming Rome, or was blacked out altogether while the thunder lasted, or flared white with the lightning. Through all these extremes of heat and shade and light I clung to Mamma, protesting loudly that I was not frightened.

Mamma had taken three tickets and I was deputizing for a friend. Her other guest was Sir Hedworth Williamson, who appeared to treat the appalling scene in front of him with comforting levity. Gradually, I too began to scoff at it as being 'only a play'.

In the row of stalls behind us a lady arrived late. At that moment the stage was at its blackest and the thunder at its most loud. Blindly, she groped her way into her seat. Then she took the long pins out of her hat, removed her hat and pinned it to the back of the seat in front of her.

A scream, not from Agrippina, rang out by my side. On the stage the lightning flared, and by its light I beheld the terrifying spectacle of Sir Hedworth Williamson impaled, like a gigantic butterfly, on the back of his seat. And a doctor had to be sent for to dress the wound and to treat him for shock.

Needless to say, the psychiatrist added this episode to my first important impressions. And, inevitably, from it I derived a lifelong fear of thunder and lightning, and a dream-ridden fear of being stabbed in the back. Almost, my reactions seemed too obvious: following rubber-stamp psychiatry?

Very carefully, Mamma chose my next play: 'Mother Goose'.

Usually, expeditions with Mamma took an exciting turn.

Those I liked best were on foot, especially the one which led us across Hyde Park to the Westminster Bank, near Albert Gate.

Mamma walked with the tirelessness of a Scots gillie, and Papa said that she should have been the mascot of his Yeomanry regiment. It was difficult for me to keep up with her, but somehow I did. To earn her good opinion, nearly everyone who knew her made a superhuman effort. And cupidity lent extra strength to my fat legs on our expeditions to the Westminster Bank.

Throughout her life, Mamma was irresistibly attractive to bank managers, and the one at Albert Gate was as infatuated as the rest. On our arrival, Mr. Montagu would be hovering near the doorway, ready to bow us into his inner sanctum. Once inside it, he would place Mamma opposite him, with myself between them, and make his opening remarks in a reverently low voice, as though he was praying in church.

Usually, whatever the season, Mamma was veiled. Placing her umbrella, or parasol, on the table, then she would lift her veil, and Mr. Montagu seemed to catch his breath a little as he beheld her beautiful face.

These preliminaries bored me slightly, but were worth going through, in anticipation of the treat that followed.

From her purse, Mamma would pick out a golden sovereign and, very apologetically, she would ask Mr. Montagu: 'Would it be a very great trouble to change this, for Sonia, into threepenny bits?' 'Not at all, not at all; a pleasure!' insincerely Mr. Montagu would aver. And then, no doubt anxious to get rid of me, he would entrust me to the care of the cashier outside whom, gloatignly, I would watch count out eighty threepenny bits and shovel them into a pink canvas bag.

With the bag clutched in my hand, my miser's instinct was uppermost. On our return journey (usually by hansom-cab), I was apprehensive of losing it; and on our return home, invariably I hid it. Once, when I had overheard Papa say that he was facing a financial crisis, Nannie discovered me hastily re-hiding my booty under my doll's mattress.

Very rarely, Mamma's expeditions took a gently disciplinary turn.

Sometimes, Lord Alington took her for drives in his beautiful carriage. In the summer, to Hampton Court, Richmond Park, Kew. In the winter, to picture-galleries and antique-shops and exhibitions. He was tremendously proud of his friendship with her, and delighted at being seen in her company.

On one rather dull day, he called for her, and, as usual, asked her where he should drive her. 'Hoxton, please,' she said.

Hoxton was a poor slum in East London where Lord Alington owned a lot of property. Hitherto, he had not visited it and, as can be imagined, he was not enthusiastic to do so. But Mamma insisted.

From her subsequent description, the drive was funereal. Along dreary streets the horses clopped slowly, the smart equipage jeered at or sullenly watched, by dull-eyed men and women and miserably-clad children. Through an occasionally open doorway, the inmates of the carriage got a glimpse of disheartening squalor. Many of the window-frames had lost their glass, and the holes had been stuffed up with old rags or newspaper, or just left empty. The afternoon was cold and rather foggy, and few of the chimneys boasted smoke. Altogether, the drive took three hours and, at the end of it, Lord Alington was speechless and miserable. As he dropped her at home, Mamma thanked him enthusiastically. 'I do think it was charming of you to let me see Hoxton as it is *now*,' she said.

'Next time I go there, I shan't recognize it.' I hope she was right.

Our Christmas walk down Oxford Street was my annual delight. Everything seemed to enhance our intimacy, the jostling crowds that necessitated my clinging close to Mamma's arm, the cold wind which made her hold one of my hands in her muff, the brightly lit shops for us to enjoy together.

Just before Stratford Place, a lovely toy-shop (Morrell's) used to blaze with brilliant toys and frosted strands of tinsel. Usually, in the middle of its window was a Christmas-tree hung with candles and crackers and toys, and surmounted by a fairy doll wearing a tinsel crown, and holding a wand with a star on it. All round the tree, the best dolls were displayed in boxes, in beds, in perambulators. Unwinkingly, their smiling pink faces would stare out at the passers-by, their little pink hands held out in welcome. And, together, Mamma and I would view them, I with a delicious, anticipatory thrill that one of them might become mine, in a minute.

One Christmas expedition, we had got to this stage in our walk and already my eyes were riveted on an exquisite baby-doll, of seraphic sweetness, dressed in a long, frilled jacket and swansdown-trimmed bonnet. She lay with her eyes closed, with her long, black lashes like a velvet fringe on her waxen cheeks. Almost, she seemed to be breathing.

Standing beside us was a little girl of about my age, raggedly dressed and dirty. Like me, intently she was watching the baby-doll. Now and then she ejaculated: 'Ooh! Ain't she a beauty!'

Mamma asked her: 'Which one do you mean?' And, impatiently, the child replied: 'The biby, o'course.'

The unexpected turn of events left me stupefied. Leaving me on the pavement, with bewildering speed, Mamma went into the shop, bought the doll and came out with it, still as it was, without its wrappings. Instinctively, the child lifted up her thin, little arms for it, and Mamma laid the doll in them. Smiling down at her, she said: 'Call her Alice.'

Without a word of thanks, the child gaped up at her. Then, clutching her beautiful prize to her threadbare bosom, she took to her heels and legged it down the street.

Mischievously, Mamma looked down at me, purple and furious. 'I thought she needed it more than you did.'

Ceres again, this time in furs.

Chapter Three

HOLIDAY VARIETY

A S WE lived in London, Violet's and my holidays
mainly were dependent on invitations from our parents'
relations and friends.

At first, the Christmas holidays seemed to have a movable
background. At the age of three, I spent them at Gopsall, where
lived Lord and Lady Howe, and where I have no recollection
of anything except of an enormous grown-up, fancy dress
dinner-party on Christmas Eve. To this I was brought down,
dressed up as an Admiral of the Fleet (impersonating my great-
uncle, Sir Harry Keppel, whom I was said to resemble). My
uniform was perfect in every detail, including the sword. But
it was hot and smelt nasty, and my white, cotton-wool eyebrows and side-whiskers were gummed on, and were most
painful to pull off. Violet was dressed as a Bacchante, and
Mamma and Lord Herbert Vane-Tempest were got up as a
pair of immense twins, pushed into the room in an enormous,
double perambulator by Papa, as a very hirsute nurse. I
remember an alarming collection of Turks and Chinamen and
Eastern houris and Watteau shepherdesses. I felt like Gulliver
in Brobdingnag. And, the minute I sat down to dinner (as one
Admiral to another), I fell asleep with my head in Lord Charles
Beresford's lap.

And I remember an alarming Christmas spent at Rufford
Abbey, given over to a snob's gallery of ghosts. One, 'the
Cuddling Baby', particularly affected me. Indiscreetly, and
perhaps revengefully, my nursery-maid told me that Nannie

might find it in her bed. My reaction was immediate: 'In Nannie's bed! It wouldn't dare!' And, apparently, I was right.

Gradually, the pattern of our holidays became established and varied little, for many years to come. Christmas was spent at Crichel, Lord and Lady Alington's country house; New Year was spent at Melbury, where lived Lord and Lady Ilchester; Easter was spent at Biarritz; and the summer holidays were spent at Duntreath Castle in Stirlingshire, Uncle Archie Edmonstone's and Mamma's old home.

Where, in 38 Portman Square, my feeling of dread could be condensed into an hour or two, Christmas at Crichel meant nearly a week of Loïs's simian torments, and the yearly prospect of it was made only tolerable by mercenary thoughts of the presents I would receive on Christmas Day.

In her lazy way, Lady Alington was extremely generous, but her standards of extravagance were such that some of her guests were at pains to live up to them.

At grown-up level, she decreed that the ladies in her Christmas party must all be given jewellery which, if not actually wearable, had to take the form of animals or little trees and flowers, made in semi-precious stones by Fabergé. From such standards two results obtained: those who could not afford them refused their next invitation to spend Christmas at Crichel; those who were fortunate enough to receive such gifts, after the lapse of a year or two, economically passed them round again, sometimes absentmindedly back to the original donor. As the house-party very often numbered between twenty and thirty guests, and as each member of it had to receive a present, the shuttle-service of giving and receiving must have taken up most of Christmas Day. For the more important male guests, gold seemed to be the standard. Then, down the scale of social standing, leather: then, wood.

At their Christmas parties, punctiliously the Alingtons catered for their friends' children, but more in the category of extra Christmas luggage than anything else. Where extra cupboard-space was allotted to the ladies for their numerous dresses, and to the gentlemen for their guns and cartridge-cases, so rooms were allotted to their children. But their hosts' responsibilities to the children stopped there. What they set out to do was to give their own contemporaries a good time. Elaborate shooting-parties took up each day, and each night Loïs and I would peer through the banisters to see the glittering cavalcade go down to dinner. Moving like Paris and Diana, eagerly I would espy my own beautiful parents and, no doubt, Loïs viewed her mother's majestic progress with equal pride. (Poor Lord Alington's progress was less impressive as he had hammer-toes). But the cavalcade was as remote from us children as a stage procession, and we were allowed to watch it only by courtesy of the management. It had nothing to do with our ordinary nursery lives. Occasionally, it passed near enough to touch us but, for me, always this was an alarming experience, like suddenly being called out of the audience to help the conjurer. It was much better at a distance, where it did not notice us.

Unfortunately, twice daily, Lady Alington decreed that Loïs and I should appear downstairs. First of all, after luncheon, when we had to make the round of the table, shaking hands with each guest. Secondly, after tea, when, prickily frilled in white with pink sashes, we were expected to come down 'to amuse the guests'. Nothing was arranged for our entertainment, and the first part of the evening usually was spent in pillow-fights between Loïs and her mother's male guests, carried out with the best cushions. Excited by these, then Loïs would turn on me, and the calf-baiting would begin, probably with odds on bets being laid on Loïs. These bouts only took place in Mamma's absence and were never attempted when she was there, resulting from one glorious evening when she rescued me from Loïs's particularly vindictive pinching, and told her that, if she did it again, she would stamp on her toe. Unbelievingly, Loïs did it again. Mamma stamped, accurately and hard, and Loïs was carried, screaming, from the room.

The church at Crichel was in the garden, and on Christmas

morning, about thirty people would stream into it from the house. Like the waves of the sea, they engulfed the little church, and many of the villagers must have been squeezed out of it. The family pews had high doors and were upholstered in crimson velvet, with comfortably-padded seats. By standing on a footstool, I could see out. Otherwise, I felt like a needle in an enormous work-basket, in great danger of being mislaid.

On Christmas Day, the children had luncheon in the dining-room. Confronted by a mass of knives and forks and glasses, I felt like a juggler, without his skill. The food was disguised beyond all hope of my recognition. And each year my sense of panic returned as the footmen shut the shutters and plunged the dining-room into darkness before the flaming plum pudding appeared.

Christmas afternoon, usually we made an expedition to Lady Alington's White Farm. Here, everything was supposed to be white: animals, buildings and dairy. But Nature seemed to take an urchin's pleasure in bespattering everything with mud just before Lady Alington's party arrived. Alone, the dairy maintained its pristine whiteness, with the yellow cream and butter showing up the better the gleaming blue-and-white porcelain bowls.

Pusillanimously, I spent the rest of the week trying to avoid rows, and the consequence of rows, with Loïs. And towards the end of the week, usually there were theatricals or children's parties at St. Giles, or Kingston Lacey.

To these we were taken by horse-drawn brougham. Had I lived at the time of the French Revolution and been considered aristocratic enough to go to the guillotine, I know that I would have disgraced my passage there in a tumbrel by being sick: the same in a brougham. The vibration of the rubberless wheels on the road seemed to go straight to my bowels; and the combined smells of horse flesh, old leather and stale pipe smoke attacked my spleen. Sometimes I was sick on my way to the parties, sometimes when I arrived. (Once, I was sick into an Adam urn in the front hall at St. Giles). Nobody seemed to

be perturbed by my weakness; neither was I. Always, Lady
Shaftesbury and Mrs. Bankes gave me the warmest welcome.
But I suspect that, knowing I was coming, already they had
seen to it that my place at tea or theatricals was nearest the door.

Towards the end of the week my spirits rose as, very soon,
we would be at Melbury which I loved like my home.

Had Lord Ilchester (Stavey) lived in the sixteenth century,
he would have been painted by Titian. He had black hair and
immense dark eyes, bequeathed to his daughter. (She, Mary
Fox-Strangways, was three years younger than I and, younger
again, were her two brothers, Harry and John).

With her glowing, kind looks, Lady Ilchester would have
been painted by Hoppner, and against her own enchanted
background of beech trees, and parkland, and distant beautiful
house.

I loved this magnanimous couple second only to my father
and mother. Never did I feel shy with them or in any way alien
to their own family. From the moment of my admittance into
their house, I settled into it as confidently as a puppy into its
basket.

Straight from the Alingtons' terrifyingly anonymous household, joyfully I greeted my friends at Melbury. The family first
and its dogs. Then Mrs. Bonner (in charge of the nursery);
Mr. Gould (in charge of the pantry); Mrs. Hill (in charge of
the house). Each member had to be visited and checked over,
for fear that one might be missing. But from year to year, the
household at Melbury seemed impervious to change or disaster.

Each morning opened up the delightful routine of real
country life. Usually, there were other children staying at
Melbury, and the day would start with a delicious nursery
breakfast for about nine or ten children, at which we all ate
enormously and drank cupfuls of rich Jersey milk. Years after,
I was asked to name my favourite scent: 'Chypre? Chanel
No. 5?' With the olfactory delights of Melbury breakfasts still
in my nostrils, unhesitatingly I answered: 'Fried bread!'

PAPA INTRODUCING MAMMA TO HIS FAMILY,
1891

MAMMA, AGED 18

At Melbury, the Alington hospitality was put into reverse. The grown-ups were treated with scrupulous fairness, but the children (and dogs) were given prime place. In invading hordes they visited Mr. Samways and the horses; the swans on the lake; the deer in the park. Together with the rest of the animal life on the estate, they roamed round, tamed and happy, knowing that, within the huge park that confined them, they were safe.

Let us hope that no one allergic to children or dogs ever set foot in Melbury. Had he done so, his stay must have been brief. True, Stavey's sitting-room was 'out of bounds' to the children, but the drawing-room (that amphitheatre of sardonic, adult laughter at Crichel), large though it was, was so encumbered with dog-baskets, and children's games spilling out from under tables, that only a small space in front of the fire was left free. And, within a matter of minutes, this space, too, was contested and conquered by four enormous golden retrievers.

As at Crichel, Mary and I were 'dressed up to go down' each evening. But the similarity stopped there. Every ingenious game was evolved for our amusement, and most of the adult guests were pressed into our service. By the end of the evening, only one or two stalwarts still remained on their island, near the fireplace. The others had admitted defeat and taken flight.

Parties at Melbury were given in plenty, attended by children from the surrounding houses and villages. And in return, often we were invited back. The doors of hospitality swung to and fro, and the quality of the entertainments provided never was criticized.

The culminating amusement of each day was in the nursery-bath, which had a lid on it, casually laid back against the wall. As this provided the risk of total eclipse, it gave our ablutions a particular thrill. The bath itself was filled with toy battleships and boats and floating animals, added to by successive generations of children and, apparently, never cleared out. Like sea-monsters we sat, swamping flotillas of sailing-ships and dreadnoughts, until the last drop of water gurgled through the plug-hole and beached the lot.

Even now, New Year's Day in Melbury Church is still fresh in my mind. Lady Ilchester played the organ and, somehow, her doing so made the service even more reassuring and homely. At Melbury, no high pews divided the inhabitants of the big house from the villagers. And every member of the congregation was encouraged to sing with conviction.

> 'To Thee we come, O gracious Lord,
> The new-born year to bless;
> Defend our land from pestilence;
> Give peace and plenteousness.'

In such surroundings, even the fear of pestilence was softened by our childish confidence in the unfailing powers of Mrs. Bonner's liquorice lozenges, and Nannie's 'Pomade Divine'.

The time came for me to begin lessons, and, simultaneously, garrison-sports started, with my defenceless body as the hapless hazard between Nannie and Moiselle.

For as long as she dared, Nannie played a back-line holding game, but Moiselle was quicker, and Mamma, as umpire, usually conceded her the point.

The schoolroom was a dreary room after my bright day-nursery. It looked out on to colourless backs of houses, and through it rattled an aggressively bellicose pipe. No one seemed to know the pipe's source or destination and, some days, it rattled worse than others. It added a martial emphasis to my first lessons, as though Moiselle had hidden reserves of troops at sabre-drill which she could call to her aid if I proved obdurate.

Moiselle's most alarming factor was her alliance with my sister, Violet, who, for the first ten years of my life, viewed me with an expression of unmitigated dislike. Servilely, I tried to bridge the gap between us with little offerings, but she remained incorruptible. And, with one terrifying exception, I cannot recall one spoken word from her during that decade of time.

Violet's way of life seemed very different from mine. She dressed and walked slowly, and wore a hideous shirt with a collar and tie. Unlike me, she loved learning, and showed notable talent at drawing. She seldom smiled. And it was plain that she had the lowest opinion of my intelligence, except as an irritant. With my wits sharpened by the instinct of self-preservation, I harried her as much as I dared. But, in the schoolroom, it was obvious that her plus and my minus talents were incompatible, and soon she elected to attend Miss Wolff's day-school in South Audley Street.

Moiselle's main attribute was that she taught me to read books about naughty children, in French—*Les Malheurs de Sophie, Les Petites Soeurs de Trott*. Delightedly, I followed Sophie's irrepressible escapades, and by so doing, unconsciously learnt quite a lot of French. I learnt very little English, and no arithmetic. And both Moiselle and I dismissed *Little Arthur's History of England* as old-fashioned and dry.

Against the country of her adoption Moiselle maintained a grudge. Whereas England had not been invaded since 1066, France need only look back thirty-odd years to remember the agony of the subdued. It made no difference to Moiselle that she was unborn in 1870; or that she had elected to come and live in England of her own free will. Her resentment remained, which may have accounted for her dismissal of *Little Arthur's History of England* and her apparent reluctance to find a more modern substitute of English History for me to learn.

At the piano, her execution was refined, if limited. I would watch her square, little hands stretched out over the chords and listen to her playing, the left hand always a fraction behind the right. Sometimes, sentimentally, she sang to her own accompaniment: 'Si mes vers avaient des ailes'. Always her performance moved me. Usually so undaunted, at the piano she seemed very small and lost.

Dancing and gymnastics were considered necessary to my education and, it had to be admitted, I was a dud at both. Again and again, Mrs. Wordsworth's shrill voice rang out: 'Sonia, do that "chassis" with Miss Dulcie! *Try* to remember that it's: One—two-three, one—two—three, one—two—three—*point!*' Miss Dulcie smelt of perspiration and, if I remembered the 'One—two—three', nearly always I forgot the 'point'.

And Mr. McPherson's gymnasium was purgatory as, after the first few minutes, asthmatically, I lost my breath, and attempted parallel-bars and the 'Giant's Stride' with wheezes escaping from me like squeaks from deflating bellows. Loïs attended both dancing-class and gymnasium, and danced and performed gymnastics with equal ease. As she soared above me up the rope, sullenly I fingered my Indian clubs and wondered if I dared let one of them fly, near her head.

Moiselle accompanied me to the dancing-class and Nannie to the gymnasium. Thus Mamma maintained the balance of power between them, and peace was preserved.

It took Nannie weeks to prepare for our Easter holiday in Biarritz, as the whole of Violet's and my wardrobe had to be checked over and brought up to date.

In our youth, Violet and I were dressed by Mr. Nichols in Glasgow, and Woollands, in Knightsbridge. Mr. Nichols only supplied us once yearly, but we seemed to make four seasonal expeditions to Woollands during each year.

Because it was lucky to have something new to wear on Easter Sunday, the spring expedition was the most exciting. Colour and texture had to propitiate the gods, as also Mrs. Wilfrid Ashley's children's nurse.

Early in the afternoon, my mother, Nannie, Violet and I would squeeze into the electric brougham, and ping through Hyde Park behind much the same alluring sound which now heralds Wall's ice-cream van. Freed used to drive us, and breathlessly imprisoned as we were behind him, for a long time

I thought that his name literally implied freedom from bondage, and that Mamma had rescued him from slavery before he entered her service. Gaily we pursued our way, all thoughts of car-sickness banished from my mind by Mamma's convincing remark: 'No one has ever been sick in an *electric* brougham.' Out of deference to Mamma, Nannie sat on the extreme edge of the seat, and a large part of the fun of the afternoon was pushing her in and hauling her out.

In those days, the 'Juvenile Department' at Woollands was situated on the third or fourth floor. Grimly, the lift man shut his concertina-gates on us, and very, very slowly we ascended to our appointment with 'No. 10'.

We never discovered whether 'No. 10' had had Christian baptism and a name of her own. To Violet and me, she remained a numerical cypher that sucked pins. Always she was bent double at our feet, measuring our skirts, slithering round on her poor, old knees, and stabbing a pin into each hem from the apparently inexhaustible supply she kept in her mouth. Seldom did we see her face, but as I grew taller, each appointment revealed more clearly to me that No. 10's head was bald on top. That, surely, was enough. But the poor old thing had another disability; her tummy rumbled like cannon. Now, it haunts me to think that she might have been hungry. Then, the rumblings induced in me such uncontrollable giggles that Mamma used hastily to improvise some distraction to draw my line of fire.

Usually, our Easter toilettes consisted of new coats, straw hats and light dresses. Violet's hat was secured under her chin by an elastic band; mine was tied on by a large bow of white moiré ribbon. Both of us were equipped with black, buttoned boots. Violet wore black cotton stockings with hers; I wore white cotton socks.

Mamma turned a deaf ear to Nannie's hopeful comment that Mrs. Wilfrid Ashley's children had real lace on their knickers. Cheerfully she parried it: 'Mrs. Ashley can afford it; I can't.'

For our journey to Biarritz, Violet's and my luggage ranged from a large trunk each, a smaller trunk for Nannie, a medicine-chest, several baskets and a 'hold-all'. This last was made of waterproofed tartan material, and seemed to contain anything casually rolled up in it at the last moment. Individually, Violet and I each carried a little bag with bottles in it. My bottles were filled by Nannie with: 'Oh! Dick! Alone!', against sea-sickness. And, inevitably, as well as the bag, I carried my doll, Julie.

Pride of place on the journey went to Mamma's luggage. Studded wardrobe-trunks, standing up on end, and high enough to stand in; hat-boxes; shoe-boxes; rugs; travelling-cushions; her travelling jewel-case. The 'big' luggage went in the van, but Miss Draper was in charge of the 'small' luggage, and most of the journey she spent frantically lurching from her compartment to ours, checking on items which, temporarily, she had mislaid.

On our Easter holiday, Moiselle was left behind, and Nannie and Miss Draper came with us and, I think, a courier. At Victoria, a special carriage was reserved for us; and a special cabin on the boat. And at Calais, Mamma was treated like royalty. The 'Chef-de-Gare' met her and escorted us all through the Customs, and the car-attendant on the train hovered over her like a love-sick troubadour.

From Calais, we had double-berthed sleepers: Nannie and Violet in one; Mamma and I in another. During the day, the berths were pushed up, and we sat in large, fawn-covered armchairs, topped by antimacassars with someone's initials 'P.L.M.' in lace, written on them. Disappointingly, Mamma disliked eating in the restaurant-car, so that thrill was denied us, and we ate from baskets in our compartments.

Sometimes, Violet and I changed places and I sat with Nannie. Both she and I viewed the French landscape with disfavour. Nannie disliked the tall, French poplars and differently-coloured French houses and the flat, hedgeless countryside. ('Nothing private'). And, to me, the strangeness of it made it alarming. At Calais, not even the dogs understood what I said; and the children stared at me in open-mouthed astonishment.

But, back in Mamma's compartment, she and Violet were happy. Mamma and the French loved each other, and Violet, too, seemed to galvanize on French soil. From lead she became mercury, laughing and vivacious. I hardly recognized her, and Nannie viewed her metamorphosis with the deepest suspicion.

The only times in my life that I did not enjoy my mother's society were on those night-journeys to Biarritz.

Throughout her life, Mamma wore her beauty without vanity, as unconcernedly as she would an old mackintosh. Now, aesthetically, acutely I minded the way she obliterated it for the night. Out of a square, silk case she brought a small pillow, a shapeless nightgown and a mob-cap. Under the nightgown she subdued her beautifully curved body. And, under the cap, she piled her shining, chestnut hair. Next, she greased her face. Then, she helped me up the ladder to my upper berth and kissed me 'good night'. Lastly, she took a strong sleeping-pill, put on black night-spectacles, and lay for dead till morning.

I dared not move, and any inclination to go to the lavatory had to be controlled until daylight filtered through the shuttered window. And, even then, I was terrified I would fall down the ladder and wake Mamma. So I lay through the night, rigid and wakeful, listening to the creaks and groans of the 'wagon lits', as they rushed through the darkness. With Julie clutched in my arms, I listened to the strange, French noises. The train whistle had an hysterical, female sound; and cannibals seemed to be shrieking and stamping in the stations at which we stopped. Sometimes, I would peer over the edge of my berth at Mamma and, in the weird, blue ceiling-light, her white face, with its black-bandaged eyes, looked ghastly.

Gradually, light oozed through the shutters, and, with it, the sounds became less menacing. A cock crowed; a dog barked; and, finally, the car-attendant knocked on the door, bringing us hot 'croissants' and blue cups of steaming, hot coffee.

The last part of the journey ran along the coast and, as always, my spirits rose as I looked at the sea.

Our host in Biarritz was Sir Ernest Cassel, who yearly rented the Villa Eugénie, presumably from the French Government. My recollection of the villa is that it was like a large, inhabited conservatory, with carpetless floors and glass doors, and with its inmates potted about in it like plants.

No doubt designed for the Prince Imperial, the nurseries were ornate and formal and, like the rest of the villa, seemed always prepared for an invisible party. Uneasily, Nannie, Violet and I settled into them. Our clothes were hard put to it to compete with those of Sir Ernest's grandchildren, Edwina and Mary. And I suspect that Nannie put in several clandestine hours' overtime, washing and ironing, still sensitively conscious of the inferior quality of the lace on our knickers. Sometimes, Sir Ernest's great-niece was there too; but Marjorie Jenkins's wardrobe was simpler, and more in keeping with ours.

Sir Ernest's sister kept house for him, and his delicate daughter (Mrs. Wilfrid Ashley) was always at Biarritz, together with her children, Edwina and Mary. Sir Ernest was a widower, and his sister's husband also appeared to be dead. A catty friend said that when Sir Ernest wanted his own way, he got it. He wanted his sister to keep house for him; and he had not wanted her husband. Whether widowed or not, her docile obedience to her brother had almost a Biblical quality.

In fact, Sir Ernest was fervently served by all his female relations, and his approbation or disapproval governed their day. Vaguely reminiscent of the Genie in 'Aladdin', suddenly he would appear in the nursery, inscrutably puffing at his cigar. At sight of him, Edwina and Mary and Marjorie would spring to their feet, while, at a distance, still unable to distinguish between him and his royal counterpart, dutifully I bobbed.

Usually, Kingy, too, spent Easter at Biarritz, and gradually I came to realize that Tweedledum was quite easily distinguishable from august Tweedledee. For one thing, Tweedledee laughed more easily and, as I already knew, he could enter into nursery games with unassumed enthusiasm. Always, he was accompanied by his dog, Caesar, who had a fine disregard for the villa's curtains and chair-legs, but a close personal regard for me.

As at Crichel at Christmas, Easter Sunday at Biarritz was an occasion for giving beautiful presents. And not only to the grown-ups. Still, I have lovely little jewelled Easter eggs given me by Kingy and Sir Ernest, particularly an exquisitely midget one in royal blue enamel, embossed with a diamond 'E', and topped by a tiny crown in gold and rubies.

Beach parties and parties with other children took up our time, and on Easter Sunday, Kingy, ourselves and a host of others set forth for a mammoth picnic.

Kingy liked to think of these as impromptu parties, and little did he realize the hours of preliminary hard work they had entailed.

First, his car led the way, followed by others containing the rest of the party. Then the food, guarded by at least two footmen, brought up the rear.

Kingy spied out the land for a suitable site and, at his given word, we all stopped, and the footmen set out the lunch. Chairs and a table appeared, linen table-cloths, plates, glasses, silver. Every variety of cold food was produced, spiced by iced cup in silver-plated containers. Everything was on a high level of excellence, except the site chosen.

For some unfathomed reason, Kingy had a preference for picnicking by the side of the road. On Easter Day, inevitably, this was packed with carriages and the first motor-cars, all covered with dust, and when we parked by the roadside, most of the traffic parked with us.

Much of Kingy's enjoyment of these picnics was based on his supposed anonymity and, delightedly, he would respond to an assumed name in his deep, unmistakable voice, unaware that most of the crowd was playing up to him.

Usually, our stay in Biarritz lasted two or three weeks. On our return journey we stayed in Paris. Here, we were accommodated in Sir Ernest's apartment in the Rue du Cirque, from which, daily, I sallied forth to contest for barley sugar prizes on the merry-go-rounds in the Champs-Elysées.

In Paris, Julie came into her own, annually fitted out with a new trousseau. Mamma's dressmaker, Worth, produced for her beautiful pieces of brocade and satin and lace. Sometimes, she was given a piece of real fur for a cap or a muff. And, each year, Mamma gave her new gloves and new shoes from the 'Nain Bleu' in the rue St. Honoré. At any rate, despite the shortcomings of my own wardrobe, Nannie could be proud of Julie's clothes.

The journey to Duntreath seemed to take nearly as long as that to Biarritz, but it had compensations. At Carlisle, we were allowed out of the train for ten precarious minutes, dogged by my fear that the train might proceed without us. During this time we were allowed a change of magazine, and bottled sweets, at the bookstall. And here, too, we took on a luncheon basket. 'Fee fi fo fum', we said, as we opened it, taking out mammoth rolls of bread containing sides of chicken. The meal tasted delicious, consisting also of the otherwise forbidden fruits of Cheddar cheese and unripe pears. And there was the fun of putting out the basket at the next station. Later, the inevitable pangs of indigestion were dulled by peppermints from Nannie's bag.

Late in the evening (and nearly always in dripping rain), we arrived at Glasgow, where we changed trains and proceeded to Blanefield. At Blanefield, we were met by a waggonette and two roan horses, behind which we sat, muffled and warm, for the last delightful part of our journey.

To this day, I can remember the sharp clip of the horses' hooves as they struck the road's hard surface, and the sudden crunching sound (as though we were driving over meringues) as the wheels turned from the highroad into the gravelled drive.

From then on, the drive became an adventure, comfortably experienced in the knowledge that it would have a satisfactory ending. Darkness surrounded us, pierced only by the carriage-lamps, but the horses went confidently forward, sure of their feed in the next few minutes. At a given point, they quickened their pace, and our final drive up to the door was terminated in a triumphant flurry, as though reined-in by postillions.

Duntreath was a square castle built round a courtyard, strengthened at each corner by four pepperpot towers. Twin arches governed the approach to the courtyard, punctured by twin doors of admittance. Each side of the house had a separate entity, but the arches welded the two sides together, like the clasps of a box.

One of the doors was the front door which led into a long, low, panelled hall, filled with beautiful plants. The lights glowed softly, and the faces that met us were smiling. The pervading smell of tuberoses was delicious. Like Aladdin wandering into the Cave of Enchantment, eagerly I entered the hall.

While Nannie unpacked, I spent the last part of the evening in front of the roaring nursery fire. Then, nestling into my comfortable bed, I became drowsily conscious of the rushing burn outside my window.

Uncle Archie's family consisted of himself, his wife (Aunt Ida), and his three sons, Willie, Charlie and Eddie. No one quite knew how he and Aunt Ida had achieved this sturdy family, as Uncle Archie lived at the top of one tower and Aunt Ida, at the bottom of another.

Duntreath, in September, was the annual meeting-place for Uncle Archie's relations, some of whom met as strangers, although linked by blood-ties. For me, the rooms were filled with many unknown uncles and aunts and cousins, some conventional, some peculiar. Charlie was my favourite cousin, my cousin, Gladys, the most eccentric. To the end of her life, Gladys was convinced that she was the reincarnation of Bonnie Prince Charlie, which led her to wear the inevitable kilt and man's jacket, and to develop a wish to visit the gentlemen's lavatory at every hotel she frequented. She, her sister and her brother were the children of my mother's elder sister, Aunt May, and were themselves nearly the same age as Mamma. But, although decades older than we were, the term 'cousin' gave them a spuriously juvenile status, ranging them with ourselves on a contemporary rung of relationship.

Another was Cousin Johnnie Pearith, who lived in a forbidding house called Lennox Castle, full of fumed oak and stags' heads and Highland trophies of war. Against this martial background were his wife, poor, tremulous Cousin Jessie, and his large, pale daughter, Lilias. Mirthless parties took place in Lennox Castle with cheerless exchanges at Duntreath.

As already mentioned, Cousin Johnnie had a propensity for falling down stairs, and this was nearly carried to the point of tragedy when one day he measured his length down a long flight of stone steps in Duntreath garden. Aunt Ida had a genius for eliminating the unpleasant and, as my mother hastened to his assistance, she seized her arm. 'Come away, Alice dear,' she said, 'he's hurt himself.' Witnessing the scene, I entirely agreed with Aunt Ida, but Mamma staunchly persisted in rendering first aid to poor Cousin Johnnie.

Eleven months only separated the births of Uncle Archie and my mother, and their love for each other had the beauty of a theme in a Greek legend. Both had a great sense of family affection, but neither emotion transcended the white flame of their love for each other. Parallel, and accepting this love, went Papa and Aunt Ida, and unconsciously we children, too, adapted ourselves to it. In most things, Mamma ruled Uncle Archie, yet she was at her sweetest and meekest in his company, and (while not always following it) she first turned to him for counsel, rather than to Papa.

Papa accepted this without resentment, and I have always

felt that it was his tact, and not Uncle Archie's, that cemented their lifelong friendship.

Together with Mamma, the rest of his sisters acclaimed Uncle Archie as semi-divine, and it says much for his niceness that he seldom presumed on their adoration. I found their repeated references to his saintliness faintly annoying. To me a saint meant somebody big and strong, as well as gentle, like my St. Christopher of a father.

At Duntreath, the dim silhouettes of my mother's diffident sisters came more sharply into focus. With Mamma, Aunt May and Aunt Jessie as their vanguard, they moved timidly behind, clinging to the shadows, as noiseless as possible. I was intrigued by their perpetual apprehensiveness. 'What are they so frightened of?' I asked Papa. 'The unexpected,' he answered, laughing.

Aunt Frances was the most diffident of the three, with a crab-like approach to reality. Once she asked Uncle Archie why her holly did not berry, like his. 'You must plant male and female bushes together,' he told her. The next year he asked her whether her hollies had berried at last. Blushing, Aunt Frances answered: 'I don't know, Archie dear. I was too shy to look.'

Aunt Jessie had scant sympathy for the nervous evasiveness of her diffident sisters. To her, indecisiveness and lack of courage were alike contemptible. To my dismay, one day she discovered my own shrinking terror of spiders. 'What, afraid of spiders?' severely she queried. 'And you a direct descendant of Robert Bruce!' No doubt her scorn was intended to have an astringent effect but, if so, I am afraid that it failed in its purpose.

Of all my maternal aunts I preferred Aunt Ida. I admired her elegance and her neatness and the way she sewed. My other aunts knitted shapeless mufflers and serviceable stockings. Aunt Ida embroidered handkerchiefs and little samplers with bright threads from a gilt work-basket. She sewed more often than she spoke, but sometimes she asked my Mother childlike questions.

At the time of the South African War, she had asked her: 'Alice dear, who *is* Majuba Hill?'

The landscape round Duntreath became familiar and named. Two hills flanked the castle, Dumgoyne and Dunfoyne. Picking our way up one or the other, daily I was led up on a stout hill-pony. The person who led me was a bald, middle-aged keeper called Dingwall with whom, at the age of eight, I fell in love.

Regrettably, my love was purely sensual. Riding slightly behind him, I was fascinated by his hairless neck, with its deep grooves, into which the sweat ran like gullies to a river. And I liked his smell, interchangeable with the pony's, of sweat and peat. And like the pony's his sure-footedness enthralled me. Ignoring treacherous, green spaces, he plodded on, in unbending boots like hooves. Sometimes, I asked him questions, to which he made brief reply. But, more often, we were just silent, plodding up out of the mists of the valley to the sunny, heather-clad slopes above us. At such moments, our intimacy seemed almost tangible. Yet, only rarely, did I see his face.

At the end of the drive was the Lodge, inhabited by Mrs. Strachan and the Master. I forget at what age I identified him with St. Joseph, but he had a bench at the back of his house which, together with his seriousness, probably gave me the idea. Mrs. Strachan smelt of washing-soda, and her hands were permanently dusted with flour. She wore an apron and carpet slippers, and her widely-smiling mouth was empty of teeth, except for one in the middle. Her house was crammed to the brim with early Victorian furniture and Staffordshire figures, probably now of great value.

Mrs. Strachan's teas were so bountiful that we were allowed to have only a light lunch beforehand. There were boiled eggs and baps and drop-scones and fruit cake and golden butter and heather honey. We used to gorge almost to bursting point. And then we used to sit on Mrs. Strachan's papiermâché, mother-of-pearl chairs, and look at faded photographs of the Master.

It had to be admitted that Mrs. Strachan's parties were more fun without him but, inevitably, he appeared at the end of them, casting a shadow across her festive table. Nowadays, he would have been a member of the local council, as he was given to making long, flowery speeches, usually of welcome or farewell.

In contrast to these delightful occasions were our dreary expeditions to Mr. Nichols, the tailor in Glasgow. Neither Violet nor I looked forward to these journeys with any pleasure. Whatever the texture of the tweed selected, Mr. Nichols used it to obliterate our bodies under it, like statues covered over with sacking. He had a small shop in Sauchiehall Street, and what with his waxed moustache (like antennae) and huge scissors, he made me think of a malevolent insect. On the days our fittings took place, we had lunch in the Station Hotel, at that time very dark and forbidding. And while we ate, the rain teemed down outside. Since then, only rarely have I visited Glasgow.

The high spots of our stay at Duntreath were our picnics on the banks of Loch Lomond. Beside it, happily we unpacked our baskets while the water lapped gently at our feet, and the stillness gradually enveloped us. Then, one of us would begin to call softly, and the sound would come back to us across the water. Then another and another of us would take up the call, until the air vibrated round us with a thousand answering voices. As the mist gathered it was easy to think that we saw spectral hosts of Highlanders creeping towards us over the hill. At such moments, usually we stampeded back to the wag-gonette, glad to be muffled up in safety again, while the sun's last rays slid back across the black loch to their prison behind Ben Lomond.

On May 5th, 1910, about three weeks before my tenth birthday, Kingy developed bronchitis. As the day went by my parents looked more and more serious. Anxiety showed plainly on Nannie's and Moiselle's faces, and Mr. Rolfe and Mrs.

Stacey (who had succeeded Mrs. Wright), and Miss Draper looked equally worried.

In my life, Kingy filled the place of an accepted, kind uncle, of whom I was much less in awe than I was of my Uncle Harry, Major of the Tower of London. Him, I identified with instruments of torture and Traitor's Gate. But Kingy's advent had always meant fun to me. Even if, sometimes, I saw him in uniform, it was always on an occasion of public rejoicing.

By the next morning, knots of people had appeared on the pavement outside, and newspaper-boys ran along, shouting bulletins of Kingy's illness. Strangers stopped each other, asking for news. The whole world seemed to be growing concerned to know if Kingy was worse or better.

Inside our house, fear for Kingy's health muted each voice, and, for the first time, I was afraid to approach my stern, unsmiling mother. My father was easier but he, too, was abstracted and serious. Nannie was my main help, but even she evasively answered my questions. As for Moiselle, she refused to answer them at all, spreading out deprecating fingers and feigning sudden deafness.

I was aware of some secret which even Violet shared, but which I was considered too young to understand. This hurt me dreadfully. I could keep a secret better than my sister. Yet no one thought me old enough to be entrusted with this one.

The day wore on and the routine of it did nothing to alleviate my fear. I had no idea what I was afraid of, but, at every moment, I was aware of it. Too easily transmutable into the ridiculous, it remained unuttered, even to my father. And, had it been challenged, I would have been embarrassed to explain it. So, treated like a child, I acted like a child, but with an adult sense of foreboding.

As far as I can remember, the day ended ordinarily, and I was put to bed. But, in the morning, Nannie broke the news to me. Kingy was dead.

Apparently his death had set all sorts of unforeseeable events in motion. At a few minutes' notice, Papa and Mamma had left the house overnight, and were now with Mrs. Arthur James in Grafton Street. And thither too, Violet and I were to go that day, escorted by Nannie and Moiselle.

I can remember my violent reaction to leaving my home. Although probably only for a day or two, the parting seemed to be final. And, suddenly, the inanimate objects in the house seemed to hold on to me. When the schoolroom pipe rattled, it seemed to say: 'I've sounded frightening, but I'm here to protect you really.' And, without Nannie's daily injunction, now, of my own accord, I shut the nursery-gate as though unconsciously barricading myself against the future. All futilely as, by that afternoon, we had migrated to Grafton Street.

Mr. and Mrs. James were childless, and no provision for children had been made in their house. So, nothing broke its adult decorum. The hall was lined with yellow marble, intersected by niches filled with nude, classical figures. Menservants of untouchable dignity acknowledged my greeting. As we went upstairs, doors opened on to frigid reception rooms, some of their furniture covered by dust sheets. And, instead of the square, with its vista of trees, a row of dull houses blocked the view from my bedroom window.

A pall of darkness hung over the house. Blinds were drawn, lights were dimmed, and black clothes appeared, even for me, with black ribbons threaded through my underclothes.

The final horrors of a nerve-racking day were still before us. We were told that Mamma was in bed and, when we were escorted along to her room, Mrs. James barred our way. Probably, Violet resented this as much as I did as, hitherto, neither of us had needed an interpreter between us and Mamma.

We went up to her bed and she turned and looked at us blankly, and without recognition, and rather resentfully, as though we were unwelcome intruders.

This was too much for me and, somehow, I found Papa. On his ever-comforting shirt-front I sobbed out my troubles: my unknown fears of the preceding day; my distress at leaving 30 Portman Square; my awe of Mrs. James's menservants; my dark bedroom; my terror of Mamma's non-recognition. Again and again, I inveighed against Kingy's death, which had changed all our lives. Resentfully, I asked: 'Why does it matter so much, Kingy dying?'

Quietly Papa listened to my outpourings. 'Poor little girl!' he said. 'It must have been very frightening for you. And for all of us, for that matter. Nothing will ever be quite the same again. Because Kingy was such a wonderful man.'

PART TWO

No Fixed Address

Chapter Four

FELLOW TRAVELLERS

TO ME, the East smelt of melons and pepper and cheese. It made me sneeze as, fearful of sharks, I leaned over the rail of the ship watching the native boys diving for pennies. To risk their lives for coppers seemed a big price to pay.

The ship lay at anchor and, in a short time now, the launch was to take us ashore to Colombo.

Beside me stood my inseparable companion, Watty Montgomery, a tall, gawky, young man, who was one of the party of five my mother had selected to accompany her on her trip round the world during that winter of 1910. Long since, Dingwall's back-image had faded from my mind, and now my love flowered round this cadaverous, knobbly-kneed man, like a garland with which to soften his ugliness.

In appearance, Watty resembled current caricatures of 'The Englishman Abroad', with protuberant teeth, sparse hair and a pronounced Adam's apple. How Mamma came to select him, I never knew. Possibly she had advertised for a male, travelling nursery-maid. (If so, she had acquired a treasure.) Self-appointed, throughout the voyage he relieved poor, gasping Nannie, guiding me past convivial parties and cuddling couples on deck, adapting intriguing games to wind and weather and, as it grew hotter, reading me *The Jungle Book* in his colourless voice, while his bony fingers carved me out exquisite bits of dolls' furniture. Even to me, he contrasted sharply with

Mamma's other companions, Uncle Archie and Aunt Ida and, in particular, Mamma's convivial nephew, Ronnie, and his wife, Eva. Beside their uninhibited self-confidence, Watty produced rather a bogus effect, like that of a travelling clergyman supplied by Cook's. But to me, he was a giant to lean on. When I was with him, like a ribbon of paint squeezed out of a tube, his immensely tall, narrow body elongated into a mental shadow of my father, and I loved him accordingly.

The ship seemed to be the centre of a cacophony of sound; ship's bells, native shrieks, splashing oars, tugs' whistles. Nannie appeared on my other side in her general's tropical uniform; and Moiselle, like an intrepid Zouave; and Violet, with an expression of catastrophic foreboding. Faced with a new world of jungle dangers, I clung to the ship's rail, for once unresponsive to Watty's suggestion that, if I looked, I might see Mowgli on the jetty.

Then, as it seemed to me, all the ship's company appeared, escorting my mother, and most of her cavalcade followed her into the launch.

In my anxiety not to fall between the launch and the jetty, I lost a shoe overboard, and hopped on shore on one foot, like a woebegone bird, with Julie pinioned under one wing. We drove along a red road, like a tongue, to be swallowed up by the hotel's gilded doorway. There, the illusion of being inside a huge mouth was emphasized by elephants' tusks, like giant molars, ranged round the main hall.

Our first night was a nightmare. After sundown, hordes of cockroaches advanced towards us, retreating as the light revealed them, and then, in the darkness, advancing again. My love developed another devastating attribute, a pair of huge feet. Linking arms, crunchingly he and Ronnie went into battle, and presumably they were victorious, as eventually we slept.

The first stir of day shattered Nannie's routine. From then on, Mamma decreed that we should get up at six each morning. Nannie looked stupefied. But, to me, Mamma's plan was splendid. Thereafter, we breakfasted out-of-doors, where no cockroaches assailed us, in daylight.

At first, each new object alarmed me; people, animals, trees. Even the fruit seemed distorted. Melons elongated, developing black pips inside; plums became rotten, and tasted of scent; bananas shrank to thumb-size, and their flesh became pink. I felt better reconciled to them all when Watty told me that the Swiss Family Robinson had lived on these fruits and, certainly, the bananas tasted delicious. Then, gradually, custom blunted my fears, and my eyes accepted the extraordinary without blinking. I saw little, humped oxen pulling wagons, like sunbonnets in shape; and black men, between shafts, pulling white men in dogcarts; and black men wearing skirts, with long hair coiled up with combs on their heads; and black women, with bare breasts, crowned by huge baskets of washing. Giant palm trees reared up on either side of the streets, and everywhere the strange sounds and smells persisted. They gave Nannie a headache, and she was revolted by the women's bare breasts. But I found them all rather exciting.

After a few days in Colombo, in a cavalcade of three cars, we set out for the hills, to Sir Thomas Lipton's tea plantation near Nuwara Eliya. Like the coils of a snake, tropical roots reared back from the sides of the road. Monkeys chattered at us from the trees. Brilliant humming-birds darted in front of us. Giant butterflies lured us on. Like a lavish stage-set, as it slid smoothly past us, the scene took on an unreal, theatrical character. Drury Lane seemed quite near. Hyde Park, immensely far away. As actors, now all of us were incorporated into the scene. Yet still I felt like Alice, caught up between truth and fiction.

At that time, in 1910, few natives had seen machine-driven cars, and crowds of them came out to see us as we drove through their villages. As we drew nearer to them, usually their frightened chattering stopped, to be replaced by an awed silence. Driving in the front car with Mamma and Uncle Archie and Watty, I became aware of this, and Mamma said that probably the natives thought the cars were new gods. This supposition was thrilling, as though suddenly we, in the cars, had developed powers of hypnosis.

In one village, an old woman confronted us in the middle of the street. On her head she balanced a big basket of fruit. Both her arms were upstretched to the basket, and she swayed slightly, seemingly engaged in some dance without steps. Her eyes were fixed on our car and, as we drew nearer, I could see her white eyeballs. Doing about ten miles an hour, the car drove cautiously forward. Then the chauffeur sounded his horn. The next thing I remember was a bump, and then fruit from the basket flew all over the road. It looked so funny, I giggled. Then the crowd began to scream, and my giggling turned to screaming, too.

To my consternation, Watty slapped my face. 'Shut up! You little fool!' he said, and Mamma did not reprimand him. He jumped out of the car, and Mamma and Uncle Archie followed him, leaving me, furious and mortified, inside it. Dimly, I sensed that we had killed the poor old woman. Yet, still the feeling uppermost in my mind was one of self-pity. A native policeman appeared, and Watty towered over him, quietly answering his excited questions. Mamma and Uncle Archie stood beside him, while the villagers crowded round vociferously. Eventually, the legal points appeared to be settled. And evidently Mamma's generosity placated the poor old woman's relations. Like an old rag-doll, I saw her carried limply away. And, even then, I could only feel thankful she was not Julie. The others climbed back into the car and, once more, we started under way. Mamma was very gay with me. Uncle Archie and Watty were serious and silent. I did my best to respond to Mamma, but still my heart was heavy. I heard her say to Uncle Archie: 'I'm afraid it's been a great shock to Sonia.' She was right; it had been. But the shock had been administered by Watty.

The rest of our three months' stay in Ceylon I spent six

thousand feet up, which perhaps accounts for my subsequent dislike of panoramic views, except for short periods.

The fun was in the plains: the birds and flowers in the jungle; the rickshaws and fascinating bazaars in the towns.

Miles and miles of tea-shrubs, all identical, separated Sir Thomas Lipton's plantation from the next one. And whole ranges of mountains. We were part of the sunrise and sunset and of the clouds at Dambatene. And, as Ronnie said, the only people on the plantation with no urge to plant tea.

Like a crushed-in opera hat, Dambatene Bungalow squatly crowned the plateau and, no doubt, with opera-cum-field-glasses, from it Sir Thomas could proudly survey his vast estates. In the daytime, the vista was wonderfully vivid, with hundreds of native women, in gay colours, picking tea. But at night, the darkness was absolute and as impenetrable as black velvet. Only near sounds of croaking frogs and crickets broke the silence. The rest of the world was out of earshot and, as it seemed to me, out of reach.

And it took me a long time to get over my initial shock on arrival. Surrounded by packing-cases of stores; an unknown lot of native servants; Ronnie and Eva trying to find the whisky; Uncle Archie with migraine; Aunt Ida who had lost her embroidery; Violet in a mood of settled melancholy; and Nannie and Moiselle in open conflict; Mamma and Watty drove me into the garden. There, I was told to look at the view until they called me to come in again.

Like a badly fitting cape, the garden (a coarse patch of un-kempt lawn) clung to the shoulder of the plateau. Beyond the plateau it stopped abruptly and the tea plantations took over.

Obediently, I looked at the view, and the magnitude of it appalled me. Always I had preferred things under life size, which I was able to master. In this measureless expanse I was of no account whatever. Not even as important as a well-growing plant of tea. The realization of this was disturbing. So, to re-establish my self-confidence, I turned my back on it.

Something wriggled towards me through the high, coarse

grass. Something about as thick as my leg, and about six feet long. It was dark brown in colour and it slithered over the ground at great speed. It seemed to have no head (or only a small one) and no legs or feet. Petrified with terror, I realized that it was an immense snake. With my eyes bulging and my breath held, I watched it glide past me over the edge of the lawn. There, it disappeared.

In answer to my screams, this time Mamma and Watty ran towards me. And they, too, looked alarmed as I shrieked: 'A snake! A snake!'

Snakes were rare in Ceylon, and seldom seen so high up in the hills. So Mamma went in search of the native butler, for his possible explanation. To her indignant surprise, he started to laugh. 'But that is our house-snake,' he gurgled. 'We keep him in the roof to catch mice!'

I never got used to the existence of a six-feet-long watch-snake guarding the house. And, at the time, I must have been grateful that Aunt Jessie was not with us. Had she been, no doubt she would have upbraided me for my fear of snakes, in view of the fact that I was a descendant of Genghis Khan.

With the exception of Uncle Archie, Aunt Ida, Nannie, Moiselle, Miss Draper and myself, the rest of the party was equipped for big-game hunting, which paraphernalia added considerably to the weight of our luggage. The low passages in Dambatene were crowded with rifles and cartridge cases and huge nets and wading boots and cameras. Once I had reconciled my conscience to Watty's assurance that camp fires would keep Akela and Bagheera and Baloo out of range of danger, I began to envy the others their approaching expedition into the jungle, and to beg Mamma to let me go too. But the swampy heat was not supposed to be good for my asthma, and I was forced to remain with Nannie and Moiselle on the heights of Nuwara Eliya.

As a parting consolation, Mamma arranged for Moiselle and me to go for a drive in one of the pretty little bullock carts to a beauty spot about five miles away, called the Moon Plain.

The order got muddled, and in due course there appeared before the door of the hotel a large rickety cart, drawn by a buffalo, seemingly attached by its tail.

In vain, did Moiselle argue with the hall-porter that there had been a mistake, and that Mamma had meant us to drive behind one of the tiny, humped oxen, not a hippo. The hall-porter was adamant. Apocryphally, he said: 'It is paid for, to the Moon Plain.' So, to the Moon Plain we went, behind a buffalo with diarrhoea and a deaf-mute driver.

That journey established Moiselle for ever in my respectful esteem. With Gallic resilience, she rose to the occasion and, ignoring the appalling discomfort, managed to rouse in me a flickering sense of humour. Behind the driver's implacable back we lurched on, mile after mile, horribly vulnerable to the poor buffalo's pervading sickness, and totally unable to divert the driver from his goal. Mercifully for us, for some unaccountable reason, I had brought with me a small umbrella, and this fragile barricade sheltered us from some of the storm. On our return, two and a half hours later, we felt we had made history. But our clothes had to go to the laundry, and we bathed in Jeyes' Fluid.

Within a few days, the big-game hunters returned, with one dead crocodile between them, sieved like a colander. Apparently, everyone had shot at it, and everyone claimed to have killed it. Its hide was too punctured with holes to be worth curing, and I like to think that its carcass was left to rot on the Moon Plain, devoured by carrion.

In fact, the only time we were in real danger from wild animals was at the circus in Colombo, the night before Violet and I returned to Europe, and Mamma and her companions continued their journey eastwards. Here, the slenderest palisade separated us from very under-doped lions, and the audience remained apprehensively still until the performance ended.

In the same boat, and inevitably escorted by Nannie and Moiselle, Violet and I were to return to Hamburg. From thence we were to be transported by train to Munich, there to learn German.

The parting with Mamma was terrible, and to it was added my misery at parting with Watty. To this, I was powerless to give expression, so that probably he remained unaware of it.

Mamma's party came on board with us and remained until the last moment, laughing and talking. Then, for the first time in my memory, through a wall of tears, together Violet and I watched Mamma's figure lit up on the quayside growing smaller and smaller as the ship drew away from the shore.

As I said, Violet and I watched Mamma together. And, from that moment, for me the 8,000-mile-long voyage to Ceylon was justified. As we went below to our cabins, Violet bade me 'good night'.

Chapter Five

ENGLAND ÜBER ALLES

ALTHOUGH RATHER sinister, the tidiness of the German landscape impressed me. It had a sharply defined, scrubbed-up look, like an hospital theatre prepared for an operation. Like scalpels, the fir trees looked dangerously pointed and, with frost sparkling on their branches, they shone like steel. I had an uneasy feeling that I was being admitted into the country as a patient, and that I would be treated as a patient for as long as I stayed in it.

Trains again. And again, quite unlike the French 'wagon lit' and the Scottish express. These were wider and grimmer, with glaring lights which seemed to subject me to anatomical examination. However much I shifted my head, I could not escape them. And the polished, wooden walls of the compartments reflected everything back at me, as though to warn me that they saw what I was doing.

By the time we reached Munich, I was terribly tired. Nannie and Moiselle were having a row; and Violet seemed withdrawn from her recent vantage of friendliness.

The snow lay thick in the street, and the cold was piercing. The station bus skidded along the length of the Maximilian-strasse and reined-in outside number 'Five'. There was a briefly comforting similarity between the fat brass 'Five' on this door and the 'Five' on Aunt Jessie's door in Wilton Street. But it stopped there. Behind the door, a gaunt staircase reared up out of sight. And the threadbare mat at its entrance was quite unlike the springy, straw mat at Aunt Jessie's.

Moiselle started an altercation with the driver in Esperanto, in which, surprisingly, Nannie took no part. With a sudden sense of alarm, I realized that my garrison-commander had gone on the retired list, and that her captain was taking over.

Still muttering, the driver staggered up the dreary staircase behind us, carrying Violet's trunk. And, like prisoners, Nannie and Violet and I plodded in front of him. But, as our vanguard, Moiselle strutted before us with her head up, an indomitable Chantecleer.

At the top of the stairs, a door flew open and a yellow glow shone out on to the landing. Framed in it, stood a reminiscently Wagnerian figure ('Erda by gaslight?') unexpectedly draped in pink flannel. Unconsciously, we braced ourselves to hear it sing, and its rather slurred speech of welcome came as an anticlimax.

Again, Moiselle took charge, hopping like a bantam between Frau Glocker and the driver. Twice more, the poor man staggered up the stairs with our luggage and then, looking as if Moiselle had tipped him in bird-seed, grumblingly he took himself off.

Frau Glocker led us into our bedrooms where, immediately, their antiseptic character was plain. Lino floors; two chairs, a table. Muslin curtains, probably already rinsed in disinfectant. Reception beds, with one pillow each and, seemingly, a pack in the middle. The drum of sterile dressings appeared to be missing but, probably, this was decently concealed with the night-commode, behind the screen.

Extremes of temperature governed our apartments. Within the immediate proximity of the small stoves in the corner, the atmosphere was stifling. But, an inch or two outside it, our breath condensed the cold air into clouds. Double windows barricaded the rooms against the Arctic cold outside, made doubly frost proof by bolsters of cloth wedged between them. When Nannie tried to open the windows, furiously Frau Glocker shut them again. As igloo hospital rules appeared to be in force, there seemed little else that Nannie could do. The implied rigours of an Arctic winter were too much for my ebbing courage, and, violently, I wheezed.

At this juncture, Moiselle went into battle. 'This child! She die if she no breathe!' she cried. 'Now—you open the window! Or we go to the Ambassadeur Britannique!' Frau Glocker looked as though she were going to charge Moiselle and then, abruptly, she changed her mind. Very gingerly, she shifted one bolster and prized open a chink of one window. 'No more will I do', she muttered, and majestically withdrew.

A knife blade of cold stabbed at us through the window, and we were glad enough to shut it again. The first round had gone to Moiselle but, thereafter, the Franco-Prussian War was on.

Frau Glocker claimed that, in her youth, she had sung in Wagnerian opera and, obviously, she saw herself as Elsa, and not Erda. Almost permanently she was arrayed in pink flannel, as though snatching essential respite between existing arias. Her sitting-room (or dressing-room) was packed with operatic signed photographs, not always convincingly genuine. Behind many of the photographs lurked half empty glasses of cognac. Within twenty-four hours, Moiselle's alertly inquisitive nose had sniffed these out, and thereafter she stored the knowledge of them in her arsenal of weapons against Frau Glocker.

About ten boarders, including ourselves, made up the in-mates of the 'pension' and now, like faded photographs, their outline is so dim that I can hardly see it. But certain ludicrous features still show up clearly. Whatever the zero temperature outside, still I can see the flushed, perspiring forehead of the old professor, who seemed to inhale his soup through his nose, like 'Friar's Balsam'. And the obviously stitched parting of the flaxen wig worn by the lady who seemed to live on 'apfel purée'. And, most vivid of all, the wooden leg of another pink-flannelled lady. At the beginning of luncheon, the owner of this leg was wheeled in, in a push-chair, to a point of vantage near the dining-room stove. Here, ceremoniously, her leg was unscrewed for her by an attendant and put to warm in the stove's inner chamber. With scrupulous regard to hospital decency, the operation was carried out under cover of a small, crochet rug. And, with an impeccable sense of hospital decorum, the other inmates of the dining-room affected not to notice the manœuvre. The first time I saw it, I thought I was going to be sick. But, when I realized that the leg was made of wood and not flesh, I looked forward to its pre-prandial unscrewing with the zest of a whetted appetite.

We ate breakfast and luncheon communally with the other residents, and tea apart, in our sitting-room. One perfectly ordinary young man was a brother-resident, a handsome South American called Herr Bunger. At variance with his generally healthy appearance, Moiselle decided that he was underfed and, after a few days, it became a ritual for her to ask him to tea, once weekly. The preliminaries to this meal were much to my liking, entailing visits to an adjacent cake shop for cream buns and 'sand-kuchen'. But the meal itself was unsatisfactory, as the major portions of cream bun and cake were pressed between the compliant lips of Herr Bunger, and not between mine.

Bracing though it was, the Munich air did not appear to benefit my asthma. Outside, it took away my breath, and inside, as already stated, it eddied round the rooms with will-o'-the-wisp uncertainty. After the first evening, the double windows were hermetically sealed again. And, at night, I was spread out in bed under the hospital-pack, like paste thinly spread between slices. At that time, when an attack was on, Nannie sewed me into a cotton-wool jacket. This consisted of wedges of wool back and front, secured with tapes around my middle. The fluff from the wool got up my nose, but I was so used to the process that I accepted it without question. Encased in twin layers of wool, inside the hospital-pack, I must have looked like an ailing silkworm. But it was the hospital-pack that seemed to suffocate me. Although of feather weight, put there by alien hands, I was terrified of its impact. My

MYSELF AS GREAT-UNCLE HARRY KEPPEL,
1903

VIOLET IN FANCY DRESS,
1903

premonition seemed to be proving correct, and already I was qualifying as an in-patient in this hospital-country.

My new-found friendship with Violet continued, now flatteringly cemented by a conspiratorial language. The basis of it was to be as incomprehensible as possible to outsiders. As a start, we altered our names to Byvy and Dona and then, shortly afterwards, to By and Do.

At this time, Violet was rising seventeen and in process of completing her education. At the college she (and later I) attended, her flair for foreign languages attracted to her girls of various nationalities, as well as German. With these, she was far more at home than she was with the few English girls whom we met occasionally. For preference, she chose the bizarre rather than the ordinary. And, were she to notice them, the English girls had to possess some very unusual quality to counteract their insularity.

Frequently, Violet brought her foreign friends back to tea, and I looked forward to their advent with the eagerness of one who had access only to the performance of a group of strolling players. There was Carmen, of South America, with hats so large that both sides of the double doors had to be opened to admit her. And 'Satanique', a budding hypochondriac addicted to bronchial colds, who was insistent that at her side must be placed a saucepan of boiling water. Throughout tea, into this she dipped and extracted a mustard plaster, plumping it on her chest, between mouthfuls of chocolate cake. And Andrea, who was so small that only her eyes appeared above the tea-table. Now and then, a tiny hand reached up and clawed off a morsel of food, and the crumbs she left behind her would have victualled an aviary.

Having got them there, Violet sat back and enjoyed her friends' eccentricities as much as I did. And, really, our jokes about them in the 'Vuddly Language' must have seemed very ill-mannered. At long last, having achieved her friendship, I was not going to dispute the terms of it. Especially as now she was proving herself immensely funny after her decade of silence.

But, somehow, for my own friends, I clung to the ordinary English qualities she passed over. I liked the two Molesworth girls because their grandmother had written *The Cuckoo Clock*. And because, most of our lives, we appeared to have gone to bed at the same time, and to have had milk and biscuits for supper. It was fun to swap stories with them, and to find out how many of the same sort of things we had done at home, in England. And it was a great relief to be able to talk to them spontaneously in English. Hildegarde Smythe-Martin (a solid, immensely determined American girl), found it a relief to talk English, too. So my friends and I formed ourselves into an English-speaking union, limited to four members.

As the weather grew warmer, my asthma improved and I, too, joined the college. Away at the top, Violet queened it with her clever friends, proficient in nearly every subject except mathematics. In this, she was a non-starter, and tireless in her efforts to avoid attending these classes.

True to the instinct for embroidery inculcated in me by Aunt Ida, I took to embroidering handkerchiefs, usually in some lurid pattern. One had a design of dots all over it, carried out by me in scarlet cotton. During break, to my dismay, one morning, an agitated form mistress came up to me. 'Sonia! Sonia! Komm hier! Deine schwester blutet!' Horrified, I followed behind her to a dark room, where Violet lay wanly on a sofa. Behind an apparently blood-soaked handkerchief I saw her eyes, alertly watching me. I approached nearer, and the next minute we became accomplices. 'Her nose is bleeding! It always does!' I lied. And, with my lavishly embroidered handkerchief pressed to her nose, once again Violet escaped her maths. lesson.

At the college, Hildegarde and I were in the same class, and it did not take kindly to either of us. Openly, the German girls laughed at us, and stole our stock of pencils and indiarubbers. We were not apt pupils, and our non-comprehension of the

German language was the main cause of derision. Outwardly, Hildegarde bore her discomfiture better than I. (Once it became obvious that I was an asthmatic, I was the main target for torment.) But, inwardly she brooded. Finally, with commendable psychology, she decided on the use of force.

At one end of our classroom a door led to a narrow staircase down to the street. As a short cut, most of the girls used it. But, as it was very dark, the form's mistress went out by another door into the main passage. On a given afternoon, Hildegarde took up her stance half-way down the staircase while I, as the lightweight, lurked behind the door, at the top. One by one, the girls came through it, tripped over my foot and, off balance, hurtled down on to Hildegarde's waiting fists. The results were magnificent. About a dozen girls piled up groaning, at the bottom. In the 'mêlée', Hildegarde and I escaped.

Next morning, the form-mistress severely reprimanded the perpetrators of the assault, who were asked to step forward. Nobody did so, so nobody was punished. Blandly, Hildegarde and I surveyed our German form-mates, and on our return from lunch that day, most of our pencils and rubbers were back in our desks.

From then on, our classmates treated us better, and a wary amicability grew up between us. But nothing warmer. Still, the English-speaking union solidly adhered to its original membership, with non-fraternization implicit as one of its rules.

Devotedly, once a month, Papa came out from England to visit us. And, judiciously, he divided his time between Violet and me. Most of the hours of daylight he accorded me and, after sundown, he took out Violet.

Summer now coloured the Bavarian hillside, and I enjoyed my walks down the wide streets with Papa. We shopped and went to teashops, and sometimes to museums. And more than once we drove out to little 'Gast' houses in the country. Our amusements were usually lowbrow and volatile, following much the same pattern as that of other German children.

But, after sundown, Papa and Violet joined the world of Grand Opera, where everything seemed exaggerated and sinister, governed by the fantasies of the mad King of Bavaria. My knowledge of Bavarian history and Wagnerian operas got a bit mixed and, to the end of my stay in Munich, I had a hazy idea that the Prince Regent drove out at midnight in a sleigh drawn by black horses, while his wife, looking like Frau Glocker, sat beside him, wearing Brünnhilde's breastplate over her dressing-gown.

I was considered too young to attend the opera, so I was treated to a dehydrated form of it in German story books illustrated by Rackham, and devoid of music. I understood little of the German story and, without the music to stir up my blood, the pictures were frightening enough; especially those of Fafner and Hagen. But those of the Walküre riding across the sky on their horses unexpectedly inspired me to dream of future equestrian feats. At that age, I did not realize what I was missing. Nor did I realize that, learning the story without the music, I was like Brünnhilde before she met Siegfried, immature and asleep.

At this time, my front teeth were so prominent that I could not shut my mouth, and they were spaced widely apart, like pegs on which a child learned elementary knitting. Someone suggested that they should be brought under control before Mamma saw them again so, in addition to the doctor, now also I attended the dentist. With military zeal, into my mouth he built two lines of fortification. Two gold bars (one top, one bottom), with four protruding hooks on them, were cemented in, completely covering my side teeth and exposing only the front ones. The top pair of hooks was towards the front of my mouth and the bottom ones at the back, and these were attached together by tight elastic bands, renewed every three days, to guard against stretching. Under the cement it was impossible to clean my teeth and, with new elastic bands in place, it was practically impossible for me to eat. I was told not to brush my teeth and to avoid solid food as much as possible, and only to slacken the elastic bands at night. My case seemed outside the scope of child or animal protection.

I, too, was keen on the metamorphosis to be achieved before Mamma saw me again and, at first, I submitted, more or less docilely, to my discomforts. But soon, acutely, I became conscious of their ludicrous effect. Especially when Violet said that I looked like a Japanese warrior. Sometimes the hooks grazed the inside of my mouth and then, sadistically, the dentist painted it with healing unguents, and prised the hooks up tighter. After a week or two, Nannie said she felt sure my teeth were straighter (which may well have been true, as they were very much looser.) But, by then, I had begun to wonder whether I was paying too high a price for their straightening. Supposing, despite all I was enduring for her sake, that Mamma, too, found my teeth a target for laughter?

As the hour of her return drew nearer, I became more and more worried. Nearly a year had passed since we had seen her, and I realized that no longer could I clearly visualize her face. But I remembered the bright, turquoise-blue colour of her eyes, and her chestnut hair. And both these were such outstanding features that easily should I be able to recognize her. Would she, in her turn, be able to penetrate the disguise of my own grimacing, golden mouth? And, if she did, how funny would she find it? The nearer we got to the hour of her arrival, the more apprehensive I became. Almost I wished that her train would be late. But, inexorably, it was on time. And as the train drew alongside the platform, I felt like Aunt Sally disguised as a penny-in-the-slot machine.

A lot of people were meeting the train, and in the general bustle and excitement I forgot my self-consciousness. The travellers came to the window and waved. And some of them began to descend on to the platform.

At the farther end, I thought I recognized Mamma, and I

started to run towards her. A lady caught my arm and said: 'Here I am, darling!' I gave her a brief look and tried to brush her aside. But the lady persisted. 'Here I am!' again she said.

I looked up at her and, rudely, I stared. The turquoise-coloured eyes were the same, smiling down at me, a little mistily, and taking no notice of my barricaded mouth. But what had happened to the hair?

The last time I had seen it, under the ship's lights at Colombo, it had shone like gold. Now, it was snow white. By contrast, my lack of tact showed up the more harshly. 'Oh! Mamma!' I said. 'Your hair!' My own self-consciousness forgotten, I continued to stare. And even then, Mamma did not retaliate, as well she might have done, by exclaiming: 'Your teeth!'

Within a fortnight of Mamma's return, everything had changed. We had a flat, new clothes and, as far as I was concerned, a new doctor. This was because, shortly after Mamma got back, I was ill again, this time with diseases in triplicate. Almost simultaneously, I was attacked by rheumatic fever, a threatening of appendicitis and acute bronchitis. And, in that order of priorities, obviously the doctor came before the dentist.

The sick-room adjuncts piled up again. The cotton-wool jacket; the hospital-pack. And, with them, my terrors returned. 'I can't breathe! I shall die!' I whimpered to Mamma.

Her instant response was to call in the new doctor who, with three dramatic gestures, altered my respiratory future. Despite Nannie's outraged protests, he peeled off my cotton-wool jacket. Then he threw the pack to the floor and had my bed remade with sheets and blankets. And, most dramatically of all, with the third gesture he flung open the window and had my bed pulled right up to it. Outside, it was snowing again and some of the flakes drifted on to my bed. But these he ignored. Sheltered inside a steam-tent, and propped up against kapok pillows, he ordered me to breathe. Slowly and painfully, I expelled eight years' accumulation of cotton-wool and feather particles out of my lungs, and began to find that, certainly, I seemed to be able to breathe a bit better.

And, of course, Mamma had her own way of accelerating my recovery. Ignoring the pain of bruised knees and torn stockings, she invented a race. When my throat was at its sorest and my medicine very difficult to swallow, at a signal from Nannie, while I started to drink it, Mamma started round my room on her knees. With the odds heavily in my favour, inevitably I won, but I so enjoyed the contest that sometimes I let her get slightly ahead. During one such occasion, the doctor himself appeared. With no apparent loss of dignity, Mamma waved him aside until the race was over. Then, she rose and straightened her skirt, and explained the object of our game. And, to my surprise, the doctor accepted it as sensible. 'It is gut to laugh.'

Between them, Mamma and the new doctor dispersed my fears. And, outside my window, the hospital-country began to appear quite friendly, decked-out for Christmas.

Chapter Six

MOUNTAIN SCENERY

MY FIRST holiday alone with Mamma, at St. Moritz, with Papa launching us off, for the first few days of our stay there.

For years, pleasing aspects of Switzerland had percolated into my nursery. On milk chocolate wrappers; on little carved wooden chalets, disguising money-boxes; on cuckoo-clocks. One of my most prized possessions had been the model of a peasant's living-room, complete with typical Swiss furniture, with a carved bear in it standing before an easel, on which he had already painted a tiny Alpine scene. These childhood recollections blunted the sharp outline of the Swiss mountains and fir-trees, despite their resemblance to the dreaded hospital-country I had just left. Premonition gave way to happy anticipation, and I hoped that my three weeks' holiday with Mamma would be indefinitely prolonged.

Each stage of our journey to St. Moritz was a mounting delight, culminating in the toy train stertorously crawling up the last lap of the mountain, and the horse-drawn sleighs awaiting us at the station. Topping it all, there Papa met us (arrived a few hours earlier from London), with my Christmas present of a three-months-old Pekingese puppy wrapped inside his coat.

From the hotel window, I looked down on to the frozen lake and on to the hotel skating rink, shining like porcelain under the moon's rays. Prosaically but, as I thought, realistically, I said to Nannie: 'It looks like a plate.' Across the lake the mountains rose blackly against the purple, star-studded sky. Everything seemed perfect and not made any less so by having my beloved parents to myself.

But, the next day, I found that lots of other people aimed to share our holiday, and most of them were of Mamma's and Papa's age, and not mine. There was a dashing gentleman called Captain Dawson. And another tall, thin one called Mr. Curzon. And Mamma's friend, Baroness de Brienen. And scores of others, some with children some without. All of them were very kind to me. Captain Dawson seemed to me superbly beautiful. And Baroness de Brienen began to teach me to skate. But the idyllic trio of Papa, Mamma and myself obviously was impossible. Mamma and Papa had too many claims on them and, resignedly, I accepted the current theory that a child must not be too much with its parents.

Papa stayed for three days and then had to return to his business in London. So, on the fourth day, Captain Dawson arranged a bobsleigh expedition down a neighbouring run. He, himself, was an adept at winter sports and wore all the glamorous accoutrements of them, jaunty woollen cap, gaudy woollen pullover, ski-ing badges. He had a sunburnt face and white teeth and a reputation for being a lady-killer. I do not know at what stage of womanly development ladies counted as his trophies but, certainly, if I could have weighed-in to his qualifications, he could have added me to his bag. Making up his team of five, Captain Dawson invited Mamma, and I feel that she must have disconcerted him considerably when she said that she must bring me. Baroness de Brienen was invited also. And, as brake, an anonymous gentleman.

Probably, the run was Pontresina, but I am no longer sure about this. With our bobsleigh mounted on a trailer behind us, in the morning we drove up in a sleigh to an hotel in the mountains. There we lunched out-of-doors, on the terrace. And, after luncheon, Captain Dawson distributed his crew on to his bobsleigh for the run down to the valley. As the pilot, he sat up in front, and Mamma lay down behind him, with her head in my lap. I came next, with my head in the lap of the Baroness de Brienen. And her head lay in the lap of the anonymous gentleman. I remember thinking how embarrassed she must be. Our legs went through the arms of the person in front. Except Mamma's, whose legs gripped Captain Dawson's flanks, like a horse.

Before starting, very gay and confident, Captain Dawson came back and checked us over. 'Lie well back,' he said. 'And don't lean out, to see where you are going. You'll see, soon enough.' He pinched my cheek, and my heart swelled with pride at being a member of his august, adult crew.

The anonymous gentleman gave us a push down the run, and then jumped on to the back of the sleigh. We all settled back into our places and began to move fast.

I could see nothing except the blue sky above us and the white snow-walls of the run either side of us and Captain Dawson's back, like a centaur, in front. The sharp air made my brain very clear, and every object seemed to be perfectly in focus.

Like a petrified snake, the run writhed down the mountain side. Then I saw a high ice-wall in front of us. Captain Dawson approached it from a side-angle, and it looked very steep. Up, up we went, and now I could see the rounded nose of the bob-sleigh and Captain Dawson's foreshortened forehead. And, suddenly, his feet.

There was a yell, and the bobsleigh winged away from the wall and crashed downward. The wind whistled in my ears, and the ice-run rushed up towards us. And the first object to receive its full impact was my face.

Someone dragged me up and, to my horror, I saw Mamma, with blood trickling from a large, round hole in her forehead, and the anonymous gentleman, looking very green, holding his side with both hands. The Baroness did not appear to be hurt. And Captain Dawson had only a slightly scratched nose, which sight suddenly incensed me. How dared he look the same, when he had spoilt Mamma's face?

My own face felt numb, and my mouth appeared to be full of broken pieces. The Baroness tried to get them out. But in some strange way, they were caught up with my cheek.

Then I realized that I was covered with blood, and that a pool of blood marked the place where my face had hit the ice. And I started to scream with fright. Was my face squashed flat? 'No, of course not, darling.' Quietly Mamma reassured me. 'It's rather a good thing, really. You've smashed up those awful old plates.'

I remember a slow sleigh-drive back to the hotel and Mamma going ahead to warn Nannie. In the sleigh everyone assured me that, really, I was quite all right. In the snow, one always appeared to bleed profusely. And the broken pieces were only my plates. I had a heavy, ominous feeling that the people around me were lying and that only from Nannie would I get the truth.

The behaviour of the people in the hall of the hotel did nothing to allay my fears. As I was led towards the lift, I saw their horrified faces and heard their exclamations. By the time I reached my bedroom door, I was convinced that I had no face.

As Nannie came to meet me, I searched her eyes for grim confirmation. But their bland expression betrayed nothing. 'Had a little accident, have you?' she queried and I found peace.

Within half an hour a doctor and dentist were with us, who succeeded (despite my frantic struggling) in removing the broken fortifications from my mouth. One of the hooks had torn through my right cheek, and the whole of the inside of my mouth was lacerated. But my jaws had escaped fracture, and I had no broken teeth.

Relying on the healing quality of the Swiss air, the doctor said that he would not stitch the wound in my cheek, but would paint my face, inside and out, with iodine. Also, he would paint Mamma's forehead.

'Then, just to show Sonia that it doesn't hurt, paint my forehead first,' Mamma said.

And I can remember her now, sitting there, on the fourth day of our holiday together, while the doctor painted her forehead with neat iodine, smiling and gaily talking to me, while the tears ran, in uncontrollable rivulets, down her cheeks.

PART THREE

No. 16

Chapter Seven

SOCIAL OBLIGATIONS

THERE WAS no nursery-gate at 16 Grosvenor Street. Only the invisible barrier of Nannie's still militant authority, brought up-to-date, like an electric fence. Beyond it were the spare bedroom, her room and mine, the schoolroom and our bathroom. Having retired from active service, now her cosy bedroom became an informal council chamber, to which nearly all Violet's and my friends dropped in when visiting the house. On light duties abroad, Nannie had lost personality. Mufti did not suit her. But, back at home, she regained it, and now, established at long last in a room of her own, she adjudicated for Violet and me and our friends, with the comfortable wisdom of one whose life had been dedicated to solving children's problems.

Perhaps it was a little unwise of Mamma to put the schoolroom within the sphere of Nannie's influence but, really, there was nowhere else to put it.

Before Mamma and Papa bought it, the upper floors of the house had been let out as flats and, in flats, now we occupied it. Violet and Moiselle had one; Mamma had one; Papa had one; Nannie and I (and the guest) had one. Mamma's bedroom, on the first floor, opened on to a lovely boudoir, with eighteenth century Chinese painted silk on the walls, and Chippendale 'Chinoiserie' furniture. Papa had the identical suite on the floor above her, but in his he elected to keep a lot of the old Portman Square furniture. Nannie's and my rooms and the schoolroom were on the same floor as Papa's. And Violet's suite was above his but, lacking a sitting-room, one had to be converted for her out of the housemaid's cupboard on a still higher floor.

Originally, the house had been an eighteenth century mansion, probably standing in its own grounds. Towards the close of the nineteenth century, the ground and first floors had been converted into a piano shop, and now, in these spacious rooms, Mamma had all the scope she needed to demonstrate her matured taste and knowledge. In China, on her world tour, she had bought beautiful porcelain and some magnificent Coromandel screens. To these now, she added pictures, and English china, and exquisite cut-glass candelabra and chandeliers. It was as though, for all time, now she wanted to stamp the authenticity of her own taste on to the bogus semblance of taste that she had left behind, two years earlier. In these beautiful new rooms of hers, gone were the 'papiermâché' chairs, and the 'chaises longues', and the lace cushions that had spilled, with 'naughty 90's' bedroom abandon, into so many Edwardian drawing-rooms. Her taste remained, as always, subtly and unmistakably feminine. But it had lost the few frills it had ever had on it, and had become more aloof and aesthetic.

Perversely, and very unfairly, I resented this. It was too much of a good thing, all at once. Conveniently forgetting that my erstwhile night-nursery in Portman Square had had only a solar or lunar aspect now, despite my exquisitely done-up new bedroom, I pined for a vista of trees to supplant the row of dignified houses opposite my window. My schoolroom was half as big again as my old one, and looked down on to a cleverly contrived Italianate back garden, remote and quiet. But the stillness of it depressed me, and I found myself listening for the rattlings of the old schoolroom pipe. Now, the sniffs and rustle of starchy petticoats were removed out of earshot. And no longer did my nurserymaid's shrill laughter punctuate the evening's peace. Bereft of her company, now Nannie went downstairs for her supper. And, although the footman brought Moiselle's supper up to the schoolroom, the cheerful implications of the nursery supper had gone for good.

I sought for familiar objects to counteract my homesickness, and found them in likely and unlikely places. Obviously, in Nannie's bedroom, in quantity, where Violet's and my old nursing chair still held pride of place. And in the housemaid's and basement rooms. And in the bathrooms. And, again in quantity, in Papa's rooms where, unexpectedly, most of the Edwardian extravaganza had found a place, as though Papa himself felt nostalgic for an ultra-feminine era that had passed. Here the Lady Teazel screen had been installed. And the more solid 'papiermâché' chairs. And masses of beautiful ladies' photographs, all with well-developed bosoms and tiny waists. To my great relief, here too, I found the green plush armchair wherein Papa used to sit, with me on his knee, when he told me stories. I fell on it with a whoop of joy, and it was a matter of minutes for both of us to revert again to the old delightful formula.

Also contributive to my homesickness were the faces I missed. Katie's, Peggy's, George's, all these had gone. To my delight, beloved Mr. Rolfe and Mrs. Stacey still ruled in the basement. But the others had been replaced in duplicate, and their personalities seemed at half strength, like Siamese twins.

Still ill at ease above ground, I was intrigued by the new routine in the basement. Here an elaborate protocol seemed to have been established, with as complicated a system of 'placing' as on the floor above.

The 'Hall', as I had known it, now seemed to have been delegated to the twins. And (with a reversal of the social scales, for which I have never accounted) Mr. Rolfe and his Court officials now sat in the 'Room'. Vainly did I ask him to explain the reasons for this change. Delicately implying that I was trying to prise open State Secrets, ambiguously he answered: 'Don't ask me to explain, Miss Sonia. It's just done.'

One of the unexplainable advantages of our new house was that, in the dining-room, we could seat seventy. Everyone seemed pleased about this, and even Mr. Rolfe, as my mentor, said that it was very convenient. So I supposed it was.

But, for me, it had one great disadvantage. On ordinary days, it could accommodate two tables for luncheon, the big one, and Moiselle's and mine.

This was Violet's 'coming-out' year, and, as it seemed, nearly every day Mamma entertained her friends to luncheon. At these meals I saw exquisite beauties, like Zia Torby and Diana Manners and Bridget Colebrooke and Vi de Trafford. And romantic young men like John Granby and Charles Lister, and Julian and Billy Grenfell. Charmingly they greeted us, and then migrated swiftly to another planet.

At the big table, everything seemed on the same level of excellence, the conversation, the food, the wine. At ours, it was monosyllabic and wholesome. With feigned unconcern, Moiselle and I watched the delicious food being handed round at the big table, hoping that some of it might come our way, but rarely did it. And, at that age, I am afraid that I was far less conscious of the beauty and charm of Violet's friends than I was of their appetites.

When Violet was not entertaining her friends at home, she was being entertained. And, strangely enough, I do not believe that she much enjoyed either process.

At this time, she seemed much less gay than she had done in Munich. In bulk, she did not seem much to care for her own generation, and, on the whole, seemed to prefer the society of very old men. More than once I saw Lord Haldane and George Moore toiling up the stairs to the housemaid's cupboard. Although young men in plenty climbed them too, they did not seem to stay so long. Once, greatly daring, I penetrated into the sacred precincts where, at once, my hypersensitive nostrils registered stale smells of washing-soda and floor polish. On either side of the empty fireplace Violet and George Moore were sitting, in high-backed chairs. He was

reading aloud, and she was listening. In such intimate surroundings, subconsciously I felt that they were wasting their time.

Mamma was determined to give Violet a wonderful season,
and now plans were going forward for her coming-out ball.
Several hundred people had been invited, and Papa and Mr.
Rolfe had planned the service in the supper-room like a
military manœuvre. The house was full of men moving
furniture, and of florists arranging flowers. And of Mamma's
friends, sometimes helping, often hindering.

Mamma had told me I could come down for the beginning
of the party, and at first the prospect excited me. And then I
panicked. Hundreds of strange faces, jostling, crowding.
Brilliant jewels, grand dresses. Inquisitive lorgnettes. All of
them encircling and crushing one plain little girl, with sticking-
out teeth. Desperately, I told Mamma I would like to go out
and spend the night with Sir Hedworth Williamson's mother,
Lady Elizabeth Williamson, an old lady of eighty. Mamma
looked surprised, but she was too wise to ask my reasons.

To most grown-ups, Lady Elizabeth was an alarming old
lady, outspoken and tart. But to me she was as fascinating as
Cinderella's fairy godmother. Next to Papa she told stories
better than anyone. And she remembered things that seemed to
have happened an hundred years ago. To my joy, she professed
herself delighted to have me and, just as all the lights were
turned on, to be tried out, in Grosvenor Street, Nannie
deposited me at the door of Lady Elizabeth's little house in
Curzon Street. Only the rising moon illuminated her quiet
end of the street, and the front door was in shadow. Inside,
Lady Elizabeth was awaiting me, in a slim, stiff gown of grey
silk, and a lace cap. And, after brushing my hair and washing
my hands, rather formally, we sat down to dinner in her little
dining-room, a companionable party of two.

Another Christmas party at Crichel with, for me, a new
worry. The influence on certain members of it of Diaghilev's
Russian Ballet.

By the end of 1913, this ballet had become as much the rage in London as it had been in Paris and, at this date, the protagonists of it were Nijinsky and Karsavina. In London, nothing like Nijinsky's lithe and sensuous dancing had been seen before, and Karsavina's interpretation of 'Scheherazade' was voted to be equally seductive and disturbing. Many of those who saw their performance were powerfully affected by it, and some of the most unlikely people suddenly saw themselves as pagan gods and enchantresses. An exotically Eastern element began to percolate into typically English homes.

It percolated cautiously at first, usually into a disused sitting-room or schoolroom. But, once in, it flowered with tropical vigour. Armchairs were flung out, to be replaced by divans with heaped-up taffeta cushions. Pictures were taken down, and (where mural artists were not forthcoming), the walls were draped with brilliantly coloured stuffs. The same walls were painted midnight blue, or black, or garish ochreous yellow. Carpets were taken up, and floors, too, were painted and highly polished. Leopard skins and Oriental rugs replaced the carpets. And still more cushions. Tinsel and gauze curtains were draped across the windows, looped back by huge golden tassels.

In the housemaid's cupboard, the influence of Bakst-in-the-home was early felt by Violet. With her own skilful hand, over the fireplace she painted the head of a sphinx (parts still essentially housemaid). Heavy gold lamé curtains shut out the daylight, and the electric light bulbs were dimmed to obscurity behind opaque shades. The room glowed redly, as though it were smoulderingly on fire. Persian missals gleamed on the walls, and an ikon faced the sphinx opposite the fireplace. Gorgeous Persian jackets lay about on the divans, ready for Violet's guests to put on when they entered. On top of the cushions, casually lay a huge, feathered turban. Probably to counteract homely smells of Sunlight soap and Brasso, now incense hung heavy on the air. The minute Violet's guests arrived, quickly she shut the door on them. Much to my disgust, as I wanted to know whether Lord Haldane or George Moore wore the turban.

At Crichel, on certain members of the Sturt family, Diaghilev's impact was inevitable: on Napier, who quite easily slid into a good imitation of Nijinsky; on Loïs, in an improvised 'yashmak' and scarves, who unselfconsciously writhed like a slave girl; and on Lady Alington, who, with no effort at all, continued in her role of outsize enchantress. On Lord Alington and Diana and Gerard, Diaghilev's spell did not work. And the effect of these three suddenly interrupting one of Napier's and Loïs's Bacchanalian scenes was like that of three inverted Hoovers spring-cleaning their way through a harem.

Once again, the housemaid's cupboard was converted, in this case, into Napier's studio. (Where the slop-pails and brooms and brass cans were whisked off to I never discovered.) I had glimpses of all sorts of queer objects on Napier's walls, as I passed the studio door on my way to breakfast each morning. Very often, a housemaid would be cleaning out the room, and the accumulation of overnight débris appeared to be considerable. Over the fireplace, Pan supplanted the sphinx. And panthers and nubian slaves seemed to be inextricably mixed up on the walls. In Napier's studio, too, the daylight seemed permanently obscured, and the few weak rays of winter sunshine that filtered through the folds of tinsel only served to make the room look dirty.

Nightly, before dinner, a selected few of the guests were invited to assemble in the studio. Foremost among these was Lady Juliet Duff, whose mother, Lady Ripon, was Diaghilev's chief patroness. Violet was invited. And one or two young men. And, of course, Napier and Loïs were there. And, quite unexpectedly, a small cherubic cousin, called Philip Yorke. Dutifully, they all dressed up in Eastern dress, and, to this day, my childhood's recollection of Lady Juliet is of a very tall, willowy siren, in Turkish trousers. Thus arrayed, they all went into the studio and the door was locked. And I was left outside it.

From relief, quickly my feeling turned to resentment. Especially as, maddeningly, Loïs would not tell me what I missed each evening. Through the doorway, alluring strains of Rimsky-Korsakov's ballet music used to filter, toned down on the gramophone. Then, more prosaically, a strong smell of oranges. And then incense. Then someone would begin to read, slowly and sonorously. It did not sound much fun. But I had no means of finding out whether or not it was so. And I was fond of oranges. Hardly any light shone under the door, and, after a while, the reading stopped. A stuffy silence prevailed, to be succeeded by slight sounds, as though people were stretching.

Years afterwards, I asked Philip to tell me what happened behind the studio's locked door, and his answer delightfully consoled me. He had a slight stammer, and indignantly he spluttered out: 'It was d-damn dull! They t-took off m-most of my clothes. And p-painted me b-black. And m-made me hold a d-dish of f-fruit!'

Hardly worth all the trouble and expense of converting the housemaid's cupboard.

To me, by far the most outstanding social event connected with Violet's début was Mr. Rolfe's marriage to Mrs. Stacey in April, 1914.

I had become accustomed to hearing Mamma or Papa say that 'So-and-So's engagement was in *The Times*, this morning'. Such comments left me cold.

But, when the news of Mr. Rolfe's engagement to Mrs. Stacey first percolated upstairs, I dashed to the marriage announcements in *The Times*, and was disappointed not to find his among them. Anxiously, I told Mr. Rolfe that the editor must have forgotten to put it in. But he did not seem to mind.

When I realized how much my own digestive processes were going to be affected by this marriage, *The Times* 'gaffe' of omission faded into insignificance. For Mrs. Stacey was going to set up house for Mr. Rolfe and was leaving Mamma's service altogether. 'But how will we eat?' frantically, I asked Nannie. And I was only partially comforted by her answer, 'Your Mamma will see we do.'

Compromise helped to restore my confidence. Mr. Rolfe was to continue to rule the basement, and Mrs. Rolfe agreed to come in when there was a party, to help the new cook.

When the new cook took on the shape of a handsome, young, Swiss chef with waving auburn hair, I decided to make the best of the new régime.

Chapter Eight

END OF THE BANQUET

CLINGENDAAL HOUSE, near The Hague, was like a showboat, tied up to a bank of the Mississippi. It spanned a canal and, in a punt, one could go right underneath it. Some of the rooms had wooden balconies outside them, accentuating the illusion of rails, bounding promenade decks. And a small observatory dominated the house at the top, mentally transformable into the Captain's bridge. As it seemed to me, at any time, day or night, sounds of laughter and music poured from the windows. In the daytime, frequently these sounds of revelry were punctured by blasts from a whistle.

The owner of the whistle was the Châtelaine (or Captain) Baroness de Brienen, whose frequently nautical appearance fitted perfectly into the picture. Often she wore navy-blue coats and skirts, or white flannel suits; and a shirt with a collar and tie. Looped like a lanyard across her chest was a pearl chain, attached to the whistle. Although really used to summon her dogs, equally might it have been used to change ship's course, or to prepare for a landing. A born administrator on land, Daisy would have been equally efficient in a command at sea.

The father of a family of daughters, old Baron de Brienen had left a complex will. By it, the valuable estate of Clingendaal, and surrounding property, had been left for life to the daughter who did not marry. Daisy was the only sister qualified to occupy it, and her spinsterhood had a dedicated, royal quality about it, like that of the Grande Mademoiselle, or Queen Elizabeth. One sensed that she had made personal sacrifices to preserve it, and that far bigger issues were involved than just Clingendaal. To emphasize this impression of royal dedication, she bore a strong facial resemblance to Marie Antoinette, and, on gala nights in her showboat, sometimes she could be induced to give a terrifyingly realistic portrayal of that tragic queen, on the steps of the guillotine.

In 1913 and 1914, my parents and Daisy agreed to share Clingendaal household expenses from July to September. In origin, Papa's own family was Dutch (his ancestor, Count Arnold Joost van Keppel, migrated to England in the court of William of Orange) and I felt at home on Dutch soil directly I set foot on it. But it was my family's seafaring sense that was uppermost at Clingendaal, where I experienced a stowaway's thrill on arrival.

Just inside the front door, a steep staircase (or gangway) led up immediately to the first floor (or main deck). Off this opened the reception rooms and (like state cabins reserved for V.I.P.s) Mamma's bedroom and bathroom. Above, a gallery looked down on to the floor below, as though into the hold of the ship.

In itself, the house was fascinating to explore, but its situation bridging the canal was more fascinating still, and one of which I took endless advantage.

Given the time, one could circumnavigate the whole property. But, if strength of arm and time were limited, a shorter tour could be just as rewarding. Of about half an hour's duration, this one started just beyond the house on one side, through one or two intersecting canals bounding the garden, back into the main canal in front of the house and then, right under it, back to the starting point. The last lap of the tour was full of possibilities as, round about ten-thirty each morning, there was the risk of a drenching from Mamma's bath-water.

My only victim was Mr. Strachan.

As one of Mamma's first guests, he arrived early one morning by car from the Hook, and it was my duty to entertain him until Mamma was ready.

Late in life, the Master had decided that travelling (alone) broadened the outlook and, when he arrived at Clingendaal, he was determined to stretch to bursting-point his appreciation of everything new and foreign. Throughout our tour of the stables, Daisy's chinchilla rabbits, her carnation houses and her Japanese garden, like a well-oiled pianola, his expressions of praise rolled sonorously on until I felt that, if I turned my head, I would see the spool of them unravelling behind him on the grass.

We came to the edge of the canal, to where the punt lay, invitingly heaped up with cushions. At my pressing invitation, rather gingerly the Master let himself down into it, where, in his bowler hat and black suit, he could have sat for an aquatic portrait by Manet. Carefully keeping him with his back to any approaching danger, I began to paddle him up-stream. Most of our way lay through thick duckweed, exuding an over-poweringly bad smell. And through trailing branches of willow, which nearly strangled the Master. The bowler hat and black suit began to be streaked with green slime. Yet, still his pæon of praise continued.

He was no light weight, and I began to doubt my ability to accomplish my tour in the prescribed half-hour. By the time I got him back into the main canal, I was speechless with my exertions. But the stable-clock pointed to twenty-five minutes past ten and, with this incentive, strenuously I redoubled my efforts.

Under the rose-garlanded bridge of the house, the canal passage showed darkly. It seemed only fair to turn the boat round to let my victim see what menaced him. So this I did, at the same time remarking: 'Now we're going under the house, Mr. Strachan.' For an instant, apprehension showed plainly on the poor man's face and then, remembering his manners, his pæon of praise swelled to crescendo.

I shipped my paddle, and the boat slid under the bridge. For an instant all was eerily quiet and dark. Then, I heard water swirling down a pipe beside us. Thereafter, there was no escape for either of us as, the next instant, we both were gasping under a volume of hot, scented water.

It took me a second or two to balance the perilously rocking boat and, when we emerged again into daylight, apprehensively I saw that Daisy was waiting for us on the bank.

She was dressed in her white yachting coat and skirt and, like the Queen's Beasts her Pekingese spaniels squatted at her feet. Like two sides of a penny, the dual impression she made on me was confusing. I felt I was in for severe punishment, but which sentence would I get? Court martial? Or life banishment from Clingendaal?

Chivalrously, the Master saved me from either. Squelchily stepping out of the punt, he swept off his soggy hat and made Daisy a bow. 'An unforgettable experience, Baroness,' he said, 'and one for which I am much indebted to Miss Sonia.'

I felt grateful and ashamed. And almost awe-struck by his good manners. And once more he reminded me of St. Joseph, who had been a just man; and merciful.

Except for Volly Heath, the erect, handsome young Guardsmen and Household Cavalry officers who came to Clingendaal seemed all more or less of a pattern. But clearly he was cut out for a literary or art-critic, rather than for a soldier. Yet, for the time being, there he was too in the Household Brigade tie and white flannel trousers and dark blue Household jacket, possibly serving the usual apprenticeship until he made up his mind what to do with his life.

To my delight, he singled me out and, himself a writer, inquired of me whether I had any literary ambitions myself. As can be imagined, no one had asked me such a question before and I was immensely flattered by it. So, shyly, I admitted that it was my desire to write novels. 'Splendid!' he encouraged me. 'Why not start now?'

Coming from such a source, this incentive inspired me to the highest endeavour and, with oblationary fervour, I decided to plot two novels together. Although I realized that it would be like trying to ride two bicycles, with a leg over each, with Volly's encouragement I felt equal to this feat of balance. For the next day or two, mentally I sketched in the vertebrae of each novel. Then, with clean foolscap and a sharp pencil supplied by Mr. Rolfe, I got under way.

Contrast was essential. The first book was called *The Love Letters of a Chinese Washer-Woman*; and the second *Through Thick and Thin*. The heroine of the first one bore the peculiar name of: 'Little Hot One'; that of the second was conventionally named Isabel. Colour-contrast also was studiously maintained: black and yellow for 'Little Hot One'; pink and white for blue-eyed Isabel. The continents of Asia and Europe divided the heroines, but a similar theme of rape pursued them both, dug up out of the abyss of my subconscious. Lately, and surreptitiously, I had taken to reading novelettes wherein love scenes figured largely, yet my actual knowledge of the facts of life was nil. When describing situations of surrender, in each case I visualized a loveless marriage. But I did not make this plain. Some of my expressions were apposite. Little Hot One was pursued by a Chinese bandit into Burma where her final degradation was dishearteningly arrived at in the jungle, in a monsoon. In a gallant attempt to save her spendthrift brother from a blackmailer, noble Isabel decided to sell herself to Reginald Upton in the waiting-room of a remote railway station in North Wales. In my mind's eye, an infamous priest lurked round each corner, binding each heroine with hardly tolerable but solemn bonds. But he was invisible to others.

Late into the night, I sat up in bed, dodging Nannie's snooping eye, clandestinely finishing both novels by the light of my bedside lamp. Then, with the languid satisfaction of one who had given difficult birth to twins, I laid my completed manuscripts beside me on the pillow and went to sleep.

Next morning, I placed both efforts conspicuously on a table where I thought Volly would find them. And where, no doubt, he would have done so had he not gone off to play golf.

As a result, someone else found them and, by luncheon time, most of the members of the house-party had read and discussed them. Finally, someone took them to Mamma, and Mamma brought them to me.

To my distress, she looked annoyed. 'Doey darling, where *did* you get these extraordinary ideas from?' she asked me, almost severely.

'F-from my mind,' I stammered back.

'Well, they are not very attractive for someone of your age. So I'm going to burn your stories.' Firmly, Mamma said.

Desperately, I seized her arm. 'Oh! Mamma—not before,' I began.

'Not before what, Doey?'

'Not before Volly sees them.'

'*Volly* sees them? He'd be horrified!'

Dumbly, I looked at Mamma, incapable of explanation. Did she not realize all the toil and trouble that had gone to the compilation of these brimming gifts? Did she not see in them twin oblations to my hero? And could she not see that, in return, they were to achieve so much? Time and again, mentally I had rehearsed Volly's casual discovery of my manuscripts. His idle, then quickening interest, as he began turning over the pages. His vivid analysis of beauty and allurement in 'Little Hot One' and Isabel. His final ejaculation of admiration, as he put the manuscripts down. And then my supreme moment of giving, when I told him: 'They are for you.' Surely Mamma should realize this? But, instead, she had said that Volly would be horrified. Fervently, I hoped she was wrong but, up till now, she had been infallible. It was the first time she had failed me in understanding, and I was bitterly hurt.

Through the window, I saw Volly returning from his game. In another moment, he would come in and find me empty-handed. And Mamma, reducing my masterpieces to ashes. The situation seemed intolerable. And by far its worst aspect was that it had arisen through Mamma's fault.

Cheerfully, Volly greeted me. 'Good morning, Sonia. How's the novel?'

Despairingly, I held out my empty hands to him and ran from the room.

The Veronese banquet laid for breakfast, against a background of ornamental trees and velvet lawns. A long table covered with embroidered linen. And oriental china bearing mounds of freshly made rolls, and bowls of butter and cream and sugar and pyramids of perfectly matured fruit. In addition, a sideboard surmounted by tiers of silver-plated breakfast dishes and coffee-pots in antique Dutch and English silver, and the same delicately designed oriental china carried out in a dozen cups and saucers and plates. The whole sumptuous scene effortlessly re-enacted each morning, thanks to the skilled fingers of Daisy's cook and our chef, Perriat, and their myrmidons in the kitchen, and, in the dining-room, the planned surveillance of Mr. Hillsden and Mr. Rolfe.

The night-ferry from Harwich to The Hook of Holland arrived early and, to minimize the fatigue of an overnight journey, Daisy's and our cars met their guests at The Hook and whisked them back to Clingendaal in time for breakfast.

Many well-known Edwardians still led the way upstairs to the dining-room: the ladies a little more made-up perhaps, and with their still slender waists maybe an inch or two larger; the men slightly grizzled but, seemingly, as erect as before. Now some of the married couples were attended by their grown-up and adolescent children. And the whole scene looked like a second impression, by Bassano, of the idealized family photographs of the same sitters, taken by Alice Hughes in previous years.

I can remember Violet, Duchess of Rutland, rather impractically dressed for travelling, in a swathed tinsel turban and taffeta opera-cloak. In complete contrast, Lady de Trafford, like a sleek jackdaw, in a beautifully tailored suit and tiny, plumed toque. Following her, Sir Fritz and Lady Ponsonby, with their children Loelia and Gaspard; the beloved Ilchesters and Mary; Sir 'Lulu' and Lady Harcourt; my godmother, Maggie Greville, and her brother-in-law, Sydney; Harry Stonor; Topps Hartop; Harry Cust. Behind these poised and sophisticated people came the next generation: Diana Manners; Phyllis Boyd; Vi de Trafford; looking like matured versions of Sargent's picture: 'Carnation, lily; lily, rose.' And, eagerly following them, came their attendant admirers: Dick Sutton, Charles Lister, Philip Wodehouse, my own cousin, Rupert Keppel, and many more.

All this gay company trooped into the dining-room, where Mr. Hillsden and Mr. Rolfe, and their footmen, awaited them dressed, even at that early hour, in tail-coats and liveries and white cotton gloves. Like skilled salesmen, the two butlers appointed themselves in charge of particular properties (Mr. Hillsden sold the tea and coffee; Mr. Rolfe, the bacon and eggs; grilled kidneys; devilled chicken; cold ham and galantine). The cups and plates were borne to the long table by the footmen where, without a thought to the preliminary organization that had led up to this moment, Daisy's and Mamma's and Papa's guests settled themselves comfortably and started to eat.

As Master of Ceremonies, for weeks before our departure from London to Clingendaal, Papa worked out the allocation of their guests' rooms with Daisy; the ratio of their stay in them; and the detailed amusements of each day. Mamma disliked such details. (After Violet's coming-out ball, when congratulated on its successful arrangements, airily Mamma had said: 'Oh! Georgie did all that. I just picked up the cigarette ends.') But Papa loved them. He invented an invitation-book, with columns for 'Invited' and 'Accepted', and with these columns again subdivided into 'Old Men' and 'Young Men' and 'Ladies' and 'Girls'. Had space been available, possibly further distinguishing columns would have been included:

'Grey hairs', 'Moustaches', 'Brunettes', 'Blondes'. Violet had no more aptitude than Mamma for Papa's meticulous listing. But I had and, soon after its inception, Papa showed me how it worked. Consequently, long before I had seen them, mentally already I had allocated Papa's guests to their rightful column in his invitation-book, with a rigid demarcation line between 'Old Men' and 'Young Men', and 'Ladies' and 'Girls'. Arrived at Clingendaal, sometimes these columns got confused in their age-groups, especially those of the 'Old Men' and 'Girls'. But, on the whole, they worked satisfactorily and, as far as I knew, there was no serious overlapping in the bedroom allocations; or expressed disapproval for the schedule of amusements, as arranged by Papa, each day.

He could offer so much. After breakfast, bathing expeditions to Scheveningen, where we rattled into the sea in horse-drawn bathing machines, and gasped in the bitingly cold North Sea. And barge expeditions, by canal, to the cheese-making villages of Alkmaar and Gouda, where the round cheeses were piled up in high pyramids in the warehouses, tended by men and women in peasant dress. At one of these villages, many of our guests bought these dresses and suits and sabots; and Papa equipped himself, and me too, in the dress of our ancestors. And we all clopped about happily, stumbling, and then finding our equilibrium in our stiff wooden shoes. Diana's and Vi's and Phyllis's dresses suited them delightfully, and, unconscious of contrast, proudly I was photographed standing between Vi and Diana, like a modest leaf between two perfect blooms. Then Papa planned expeditions all over Holland to the picture-galleries: to Amsterdam and Rotterdam, and Haarlem and The Hague. And a fascinating expedition to the Queen's summer residence, the House in the Wood, quite close to Clingendaal, where Daisy got us in on a non-visiting day, because she was Daisy, and where we could wander round undisturbed, as though in private possession of the lovely quiet rooms. (Here I developed a strong impression that really the rooms belonged to Daisy and that the Queen occupied them,

MAMMA, 1906

PAPA, 1906

on sufferance. But I found no one to substantiate this idea.)
Last, and least, but just as amusing, bicycle expeditions through
the woods to The Hague, or to the race-course, or golf-course,
where we felt very much closer to the good people of Holland
than we did flying past them in motor-cars, and covering them
with dust. Every one of these expeditions meant concentrated
planning by Papa, with maps and stop-watches and mileo-
meters and individual lists of guests to each car. Harry Cust
called them Papa's 'summer manœuvres' and said that, were
Papa in command of the Army, when his method of exercising
the troops became known, he would find it swamped with
applications from volunteers.

But I knew that Papa looked on the expeditions as one item
only of his general planning. Billeting and victualling were just
as important. And the right allocation of officers and N.C.O.s
to their individual duties was all part of his plan.

'Polly,' Mamma said, 'can you lend us a sovereign? We
haven't had breakfast.'

'This is where the mouse comes in.' Laughing, Miss Polly
Cotton answered, as she opened her purse.

Simultaneously, Violet and I brightened at the thought of
food. It was ten o'clock in the morning and, except for a dry
biscuit, we had had nothing to eat since dinner at Clingendaal
the night before. Up to now, neither of us had contributed
much to help Mamma. Overcome by the disturbances of the
last twenty-four hours, Violet and I had roamed around dis-
consolately, now and then pressed into somebody's service,
to try to cope with the packing urgency that prevailed on every
side.

Throughout those twenty-four hours I had felt sick and
bewildered. Ever since yesterday morning, when Mamma and
Papa had decided that we had better try to return to England
last night. For a day or two before that, hurriedly, our guests
had been leaving Clingendaal. Ominously, the French slogan:
'Pas devant les enfants', had been disregarded, and openly,

8

in front of me, the disquieting news of the Germans' invasion of Belgium had been discussed.

Sudden change always threw me off balance, and, all yesterday, the usual routine had been upset. Ordinarily, our packing was conducted almost invisibly. Papa's and Mamma's luggage usually was packed in other rooms. But, yesterday, it had spilt everywhere, and Papa and Mamma had packed as urgently as anyone, with the exception of Violet and myself. Now and then, Nannie had enlisted our help, but not very often. The margin of error for repacking had been too slight to waste.

And the meals had been equally disjointed, served by Mr. Hillsden and one footman in incomplete livery, looking rather harassed and without their gloves. In the pantry region, Mr. Rolfe had remained most of the day in a green baize apron, carrying armfuls of clothes, and cording up boxes, and with a kind, but quelling, expression on his face whenever I approached.

So, most of the day, Julie and I had revisited favourite places: the bachelor's hut in the garden, where, at last, the door was unlocked, enabling me to go in and have a look round; the swing bridge, spanning the canal on the way to the golf-course, over which Julie and I had to edge our way with our eyes shut, too giddy to dare to look down; and finally, the Japanese garden, where the stepping-stones and tiny humped bridges provided an unfailing but temporary diversion. Throughout the day mounted my fear of the unpredictable future, which even Papa could not reduce to comforting terms.

Then, we had had dinner and then the time had come to leave Daisy and, somehow, then I had felt that we were deserting her, despite her cheerful assurance that, very soon, she would see us again in England. I had craned my neck from the car window for a last glimpse of her regally resolute figure. Wearing a black dress and white scarf round her shoulders, she had looked very like the Veuve Capet. Especially as, in the black tree-shadow slanting above her, my febrile imagination had conjured up the outline of a guillotine.

Hitherto, my life had been attuned to the most orderly travelling, where tickets had been produced and the right allocations had been made in return. But, last night had been chaotically different. Mere units of a struggling crowd, pushing and shoving, each one of us had tried to edge past the next one divided, instead of unified, by the same overriding obsession to board the last boat back to England before war was declared.

At the head of the gangway the purser had recognized us and, reassuringly, had told us that he had allocated us two cabins. Fortunate indeed, through the porthole of Mamma's and my cabin, I looked down on to less fortunate passengers jostling each other on deck. One harassed mother was trying to cope with two crying children. Inanely, I asked Mamma: 'Where will those children sleep?' And inevitably, purposefully, Mamma had answered: 'Move Julie and your bag to the top bunk, Doey. There's plenty of room for them to lie down on the lower bunk, in here.'

We had arrived back in London to find the banks shut (so, no money) and no food ready for us in the gaunt, shuttered house. Perriat had said that, in due course, he could cook us some luncheon. And he had brought something with him for the servants' breakfast, if 'The Family' went out. So Papa had gone off to his club, and here were Mamma and Violet and I, in pursuit of our breakfast, wending our way across Berkeley Square, with Miss Polly Cotton's golden sovereign in Mamma's bag.

Thereafter, in antithesis to the Veronese banquet, the next half-hour saw us consuming boiled eggs and toast and coffee in the pseudo-Boucher dining-room of the Ritz.

PART FOUR

Unknown Destinations

Chapter Nine

MARCHING OFF TO WAR

MOISELLE said that Frau (Fräulein) was our enemy, yet she looked so old and dehydrated that I felt that all venom had been dried up in her long since. She looked like the Albrecht Dürer woodcuts I had seen in Munich. Her slow movements had the same Gothic wooden-ness; and on her face were etched the same deep lines of grief. Rather alarmingly, like me she had asthma, but a dreadful, tearing sort of asthma, like a north wind whipping through dead leaves. It frightened me to think that, one day, I might grow like her. If I did, I hoped I would have someone like Lady Ilchester beside me to comfort and cosset my extreme old age.

We were back at Melbury, on a quietly happy visit of indefinite duration, while Mamma helped Lady Sarah Wilson to run a field-hospital at Étaples; and Papa trained, as one of the oldest lieutenants in the British Army, on Salisbury Plain.

At Melbury, I was beginning to get back my balance, chaotically upset by those first weeks of war. Smugly accus-tomed as I had been up till then to have all major disturbances in life kept from me, my first shock had been to discover how powerless Papa and Mamma had been to avert war's impact, even from their family. (With a still infantile belief in their Olympian qualities, I had half hoped that they might be able to do that). Instead, they had gone out of their way to meet it. Rupert Keppel had been wounded and taken prisoner at the end of August and, as though taking up the challenge, at the age of 49, almost immediately Papa had volunteered to rejoin the Army; and Mamma had joined the staff of the hospital Lady Sarah Wilson had been asked to run at Étaples. The sudden withdrawal of their dual support had left me gasping. True, Mamma had said to Nannie: 'Look after Sonia.' But Nannie, though valiant, was rather a blunted lance.

It was like Lady Ilchester to offer Violet and me, and our attendant henchwomen, sanctuary at Melbury and, in fact, I suppose she made the offer before ever Mamma's plans were made. There, mainly we were a company of women. Stavey had become a King's Messenger and was often away, and Lady Ilchester remained cheerfully in charge of us, a benevolent jurisdiction which all of us enjoyed. Under her benign influence, I became more settled. The war receded to a distance, dimmed by autumnal beauties in the foreground: the golden colour of the beech and oak trees; the frosty sunsets; the silent flight of birds across the sky.

Although his elder by nearly thirty years, Papa was as enthusiastic about his military duties as the youngest subaltern. Weekly he wrote Violet and me letters full of descriptions of route marches and sports and kit inspections and parades. (The plans for his 'summer manœuvres' brought up-to-date). He had joined a City of London volunteer battalion of Lord Kitchener's 'New Army' commanded by his friend and kinsman, Colonel Bobby White. In the same battalion had enlisted a heterogeneous collection of men, mostly civilians, in contrast ranging from Oswald Birley, the artist, to our footman, Arthur Smith. The cookhouse rang with cultured donnish voices and cheerful Cockney, and, on the occasions on which I was allowed to visit it, the whole battalion seemed to be invested with the same spontaneous gaiety, like a troupe of amateur actors lightheartedly accepting martial parts.

At Melbury, Mary and I each had our schoolroom; Miss Poulton in charge of hers; Moiselle in charge of mine. Harry did morning lessons with Mary and we three and John all played together. In the drawing-room, Lady Ilchester and

Frau knitted socks for soldiers, or did up parcels, and, as I see now, Violet ploughed rather a lonely furrow between us all.

Subconsciously, possibly even then I realized that she was not quite in focus in the English landscape, and that, in sympathy, already she belonged more to 'parterres' and terraces than to lawns and trees. Even at that age, like a Frenchwoman, she stuck to the road for exercise. And, on any expedition 'to see something', always she meant a house. There was no one at Melbury to fill the gap between her age and Mary's and mine. As her intellectual companion Lady Ilchester would have been delightful, being an authority on eighteenth century history and memoirs. But she was absorbed in running the estate and in arranging knitting and bandage-rolling parties, and had small time to give poor Violet, who must have had little to do but miss her friends. I made no effort to probe the cause and, with a child's selfishness, only noticed that again she was withdrawn and silent and, except at meal-times, rather cross. Luckily, she could talk French to Moiselle and German to Frau. But bronchial wheezes are common to any language and usually Frau's conversational efforts were cut short through lack of breath.

Mary and Harry were my very dear companions: Mary, high-spirited and generous; Harry, invariably good-tempered and gay. Over both of them their moods passed lightly, like feathery clouds skimming summer skies. But John was like his ancestor, Charles James Fox, in facsimile, with sharply contrasted moods of light and shade. All three of them accepted their beautiful home without question, as part of the surrounding tillages and crops. When with them, I imagined my own roots growing down like theirs, into the rich soil of Dorset, and I longed for a family link with the country to justify this sense.

The estate around us abounded in adventure. Especially in wartime, the larder was mainly stocked from it, and sometimes we children acted (rather shrinkingly on my part) as retrievers to the guns; or tried our hand at fishing on the lake.

My mind went back to Watty Montgomery's readings of *Swiss Family Robinson* and it seemed to me that Melbury was the English interpretation of living off the land. Largely, our activities were confined to the huge park around us. Here I was taught to ride by Mr. Samways on an old white horse called Christmas, quiet and amenable with everyone but me. It cannot be said that I was a promising equestrienne and, when finally Christmas cracked my head on a branch, galloping underneath it, and I sustained concussion, tactfully Lady Ilchester decided that I should learn to drive instead.

In the evenings, after lessons, I started an intensive correspondence with Mr. Rolfe in London which, to my distress, drew from him my first rebuff. Invariably beginning: 'Darling Mr. Rolfe' and ending: 'Your loving Sonia', after one or two of these epistles, rather abruptly, he put me in my place. 'Dear Miss Sonia,' he wrote, 'You are getting a big girl now, and you must call me Rolfe. And you must stop signing yourself "Your loving Sonia". It does not do. Yours respectfully, W. Rolfe.' I was brought up short before the fact of my adolescence, with its new code of social distinctions and self-control. 'Rolfe' immediately became an impersonal distant figure, handing me messages on a silver salver, and taking my umbrella from me as I came indoors. With alarming suddenness now, deliberately he withdrew into the background, leaving me irresolute and unbalanced, having to stand alone.

But his next letter brought me (and Nannie) thrilling information. Miss Draper was to marry Papa's valet, Mr. Bridger, and then she would live in her own house and leave Mamma altogether. It seemed inconceivable but soon it became true.

One of the facts of war that had most impressed me had been Mamma's ability suddenly to do without Miss Draper, and to go off to Étaples with only a small suitcase as her luggage. Now, I recalled the daily services that Miss Draper had always done for Mamma: drawing her bath and scenting it with rose-geranium bath salts; setting out her underclothes under their lace cover; kneeling on the floor to put on Mamma's stockings; lacing Mamma into her stays (as though she were reining in a runaway horse); doing her hair; pinning her veil on to her hat; buttoning up her gloves; putting her powder and cigarettes and money into her bag. And, behind the scenes, washing, ironing, mending. It had quite worried me to think of Mamma bereft of all this help. Yet she herself had taken these deprivations philosophically and never referred to them in her cheerful letters home.

The casualty lists were now a sadly regular feature in the papers, and one day, about the middle of September, Violet told me that Volly Heath had died of wounds.

Before he had left for France, he had sent me a flat parcel, looking as if it contained a photograph. Hoping for this, eagerly I had opened it to discover, to my secret disappointment, that it contained a delicate Japanese print. With it he had sent a little note: 'With love from Volly', and, though I had left the print in London, the note I carried round with me in my writing-case. I had no means of knowing whether his death affected Violet as acutely as it did me. If it did, I felt that she could legitimately voice her grief, whereas, deprived of the confessional of Papa's shirt-front, mine had to remain un-uttered. I could not risk the embarrassing exposure of this strange, almost adult, heartache, knowing that, even to Lady Ilchester, I was considered still too young to feel bereavement or to mourn.

As the lists grew longer, Moiselle's attitude towards Frau grew more and more frigid. And now, with the spectre of war looming gigantically near again, I too began to see poor old Frau as a creature of fateful malevolence as she crouched, wheezing and muttering, over the fire.

Then, luckily for me, like ivy, my love entwined itself anew around the homely figure of Mr. Angus, Stavey's agent, whose old tweed coat smelt reminiscently of Dingwall. He had a repertoire of funny stories and a devoted collie dog who could go through endless tricks. In the gloaming Mr. Angus

was indistinguishable from any of the shrubs around the house,
and, in the daytime, he could have acted competently as a bird-
scarer, set in the corn or fruit trees. Violet disliked his bucolic
appearance, and condemned him for having 'thatched ears'.
But to me, even his hairy ears were the symbols of a comfortable rusticity, wherein farmhands wore smocks, chewed
straws and grew side-whiskers, with only the vagaries of the
seasons to disturb their peaceful life.

Chapter Ten

1915

NEW YEAR, 1915, saw us back in London. Mamma's job at Étaples had become more elastic and now she could be at home for longer periods. Very sensibly, now she decided that I should give up my lonely schoolroom and mix with my own age in Miss Wolff's classroom. Here, already Violet had set up a high standard of intelligence which, at first, I showed small signs of emulating. But here I made some lifelong friends and entered into a new world of flapperdom and fun.

In direct contradiction to her real character, Enid Dudley-Ward looked like a cross Bacchante, with Titian-red hair and green eyes whose rather forbidding expression concealed a genius for tantalizing teachers; Marjorie Jessel had a rounded, beautiful face, like Raphael's 'Peasant Madonna'; and Teddy Leon I immensely admired for her long pigtail and cloth-topped boots.

For those who wanted it, Miss Wolff set out to provide a sound classical education. Although at that time few of her pupils worked for School Certificates, their periodical examination papers were set by Oxford examiners, and several future writers and women of talent had already passed through her hands.

At the outset, the intellectual advantages of her classroom passed me by, and the fascinated attention with which I and my associates appeared to listen to Mr. Ford's excellent lectures on History disguised the fact that we were busy squeezing fresh

orange-juice into glasses, under the form table. Not that any
of us were really orangeade addicts, but because of the gam-
bler's thrill we experienced in risking exposure.

Teddy had lots of boy-friends, mostly smart young officers in
uniform who sometimes called to collect her, to the envy of
the other girls in her class. Through her, I too became a
flapper, wearing my hair in the same long pigtail and saving up
my pocket-money until I could afford the same high, cloth-
topped boots. I fell in love at a distance with Godfrey Tearle,
the actor, and once tracked him through several depart-
ments of Marshall & Snelgrove, not unwillingly pursued by
Moiselle.

Outside Miss Wolff's, I had two new friends of rather
different calibre: my cousin, Rosalind Benson; and Doris
Harcourt. Both these girls had fathers of great artistic knowledge. (Cousin Robin Benson had one of the finest collec-
tions of Oriental porcelain in England; and the quality of Sir
Lulu Harcourt's china and books and pictures was equally
well known.) Rosalind and Doris were quite conversant with
the valuable things around them. They had been brought up
naturally to assimilate and appreciate their parents' beautiful
possessions and even appeared to have heard of some of the
objects in Mamma's own collection. What was more, evidently
they were surprised when I professed ignorance of these. Like
a cuckoo, I was anxious to qualify for admittance into both
their homes and suddenly, I realized that I stood in danger of
being dubbed an ignoramus by them, and of forfeiting their
good opinion, and that I had better bestir myself quickly to
counteract this impression. To Mamma's surprise, I began to
take an unexpected interest in her Oriental porcelain and to
play it back, like chess pieces, against Cousin Robin's. I do not
think that Rosalind and Doris ever realized the spur they put
on me but whether or not they were conscious of it, their
incentive was most opportune.

And then, at school, Miss Wolff herself stung my intellectual laziness into action. One day, thoughtfully she said to me:

'Isn't it odd how two members of a family can be so different? When your sister was here, she was so clever——'

I did quite well in History after that.

Even I realized that the war was going badly and for poor Violet it was becoming a nightmare. Within the space of two months she lost three great friends. In May, Julian Grenfell died of wounds, in France; his brother, Billy, was killed in action there, two months later; and, at the same time as Billy, in Gallipoli, Charles Lister was three times wounded and died thereafter. Much has since been written of the lost generation and of the irreparable gap it left. And almost the most tragic part of it was that it was lost so quickly, largely within three years.

Julian wooed Violet alternately with poetry and pugilism. Sometimes, he came to see her with a sheaf of verses in his hand; sometimes with an eye closed in a sparring bout. Always he looked wonderfully fit, like a Roman gladiator. At times, I know he frightened Violet (once, I heard her calling for help from the housemaid's cupboard), but equally, he fascinated her and her distress at his death was plain to see.

His brother, Billy, had been less intimate a friend of hers, but, perhaps because of his relationship to Julian, Violet had been fond of him, too. That Easter I spent at Sutton Courtenay with an Eton-boy cousin of mine, Peter Lindsay, and I can remember Billy, on a day of spring sunshine in Norah Lindsay's garden, playing beautiful tennis and then, flinging down his racquet, making quick, skilful sketches of Norah's lovely face. Both brothers seemed to be possessed by the same controlled restlessness, as though they were keyed up to the same moment of departure, each one with a toe on the line, impatient to be off.

And I have often been told that Charles Lister belonged to the same inspired company. When Julian died, he wrote: ' . . . a fierce light still beats on the scene of his passing, and others are left to whom he may leave his sword and a portion of his skill.' And in his last letter home, he wrote: 'I know now that I shall live. I do not mean that I shall not be killed.'

Poison gas had now been added to the tribulations of our troops in France, and in the midst of the mounting horrors there, Papa (now promoted to Captain) and his battalion left England to join them.

I had been acutely embarrassed by poor Violet's sorrow over Julian and incapable of showing her my sympathy, and now again, during the terrible gap in time between Papa's departure and our first news of him, I used my inarticulateness as a shield against both Mamma and Violet, as a dread unuttered was far easier to control.

When Papa's exciting letters began to arrive, they were full of almost boyish adventures which I, at least, could share. Later, I realized that, when writing to me, he glossed deliberately over the horrors, intent on showing me war as a still chivalrous, gallant enterprise in which men were knighted on the field of battle, flaunting their lady-love's favour in their hats. Unlike me, Mamma and Violet were not taken in by his letters, but we all three realized that, in some strange way, Papa was happy, playing his competent part in a world of men.

When the Zeppelin raids started and people began to envisage the possibility of raids over London, Mamma had the baths filled nightly with water, as a precaution against incendiaries, and moved Violet and me down to sleep on camp beds in the drawing-room.

Neither of us accepted the move with enthusiasm. Violet accused me of talking in my sleep and my slightest movement seemed to wake her. By mutual agreement, we left our migration downstairs to the last possible moment each evening, and then ran down in a hurry, catching up anything handy to act as a covering.

In the drawing-room, our camp beds were an affront to the rest of the furniture. Louis XV consoles and tapestry-covered chairs surrounded us; the legs of our beds stood on valuable Persian carpets; Chippendale looking-glasses shimmered at us from the walls. Our own reflections in them put up a poor show by comparison: both with flushed faces, suffocatingly hot in merino combinations under our nightgowns decreed by Nannie as essential in emergency; Violet, with a Medusa head of pinned-up hair under a pink hair-net; me, grimacing from the plates on my teeth that I was still made to wear at night.

Needless to say, there were no reading lights handy to each bedside, and we were on our honour to grope our way downstairs through the already darkened house, by the light of candles.

One night in May, abruptly Violet woke me. 'Wake up! Wake up, Doey!' sibilantly she hissed at me. 'I hear bombs dropping! And one must have hit the roof as I can feel the rain on my face.'

I needed no urging and, seizing up what we could in the darkness, we both stumbled to the door just as Mamma opened it. Again Violet repeated her story. 'I can't see anything in the darkness,' Mamma whispered back. 'We'd better all go down to the basement as we agreed to do, until the raid is over.'

Down in the basement an unexpected point of etiquette arose. Rolfe and Perriat and Mamma's new maid, Miss Williams, all pressed her to come into the 'Room'. But, perversely, Mamma elected to sit in the 'Hall'. So there she, Violet, Moiselle, Nannie and I repaired, in company with the twins.

The older generation bore itself stoically, busying itself with brewing tea and cutting sandwiches. Mamma appeared quite unperturbed and after surveying the quaking members of the younger generation, cheerfully she suggested that Violet and I should do imitations.

Jealously, I felt that Violet started with an unfair advantage over me in the matter of theatrical props. Over her nightgown she had buttoned a tight black sealskin jacket and, unac-

9

countably, in her hand she carried a gardenia. Her choice, to declaim Swinburne's poem: 'The roses and raptures of virtue', called forth awestruck applause from the twins.

My turn was an attempted clown's act riding in and out of the table and chairs on my bicycle. Thereby, I seemed better able to control my trembling limbs. In an overcoat and bowler hat of Papa's and his fishing-waders, my efforts provoked loyal applause from the audience.

None of the 'Room' inmates would play and neither would Moiselle and Nannie; so then Mamma decreed that we should all sing songs. Resonantly, the basement rang to the choruses of: 'You're here and I'm here'; 'I've got everything I want but you', and 'Tipperary'. The evening began to pass very pleasantly, especially after Mamma told Rolfe to bring up some champagne from the cellar.

Later on, she and Rolfe went on a tour of inspection upstairs, and when she returned she announced that 'someone' (with her eyes studiously avoiding Nannie's) had failed to turn off the bathroom tap on the schoolroom landing. As a result the bath had overflowed and the water had gone right through the best Adam (drawing-room) ceiling. There were no other signs of damage. Nannie's face grew purple, but Mamma appeared not to notice it. The 'all-clear' sounded, and thankfully we all went back to bed in our own rooms, with even me rather tight, and the twins irrepressibly giggly. A day or two later, we heard that forty-one fires had been started by the Zeppelin's bombs over London, and five people had been killed and fourteen injured. Apprehensively, we felt that the toll had been heavy.

As the drawing-room ceiling had to dry out, thereafter Mamma changed our routine. Violet slept on the sofa in her boudoir, and I slept in her bathroom. We endured this process for a few days and then, on the understanding that we should descend at once to the basement if we heard the air-raid warning, Mamma allowed us to return to our rooms.

To provide much-needed distraction during the summer of 1915, Mamma opened her house, at luncheon time, once or twice a week to a miscellaneous collection of politicians, service-chiefs, diplomats, soldiers home on leave, war-correspondents and such of her women friends and Violet's girl-friends as were available to amuse them. The big and small tables in the dining-room were again in session; with a sharp demarcation line of intellect between the two. Mamma dominated the big table, where usually it was tacitly understood that the conversation should remain on a light level with the darker shades of war excluded from it. But, occasionally Mr. Asquith, or Winston Churchill, or some leading soldier like Sir John Cowans, would be present, and then, for a second, the animated chatter would cease, and the company would sit respectfully listening, suddenly reduced to the same student level as myself.

Had I been less shy, I could have learnt a lot by attendance at those luncheons, and now I realize that some of the women present at them were as remarkable as the men. Mrs. Asquith and Winston's mother, Lady Randolph Churchill, both were seeded players in any conversational contest. And, as runners-up, Lady Randolph's sister, Lady Leslie, and Lady Islington followed them pretty close. But, at that moment, shyness deadened my wits in any adult society, producing in me a sort of in-growing self-consciousness.

By that time, my teeth were straighter but alas! my nose was bigger, developing a strongly aquiline curve which led to Violet caricaturing me as a banana. So conscious did I become of it that, at the approach of strangers, it flamed like a beacon. Violet had a new friend, Bim Tennant, a beautiful talented young man to whom I turned (with a Socratic belief that Truth must be allied to such Beauty) to ask him if he considered my nose looked Jewish. His answer further depressed me: 'Oh! no, my dear. Not Jewish. Merely Plantagenet.' Mamma, too, was very conscious of its size and had already tried to detract from it by cutting my hair in a thick fringe to my eyebrows.

When Papa was home on embarkation leave, to my alarm, she discussed with him the advisability of breaking and re-setting it. Luckily, Papa said that it was his family nose and he liked it, so, for a time, I was left to overcome the obstacle by myself. Then Mamma consulted Mrs. Asquith and my fears returned. Temporarily, she allayed them. 'You must unveil Sonia's forehead,' was all she said. With my forehead formally 'unveiled', my shyness should have evaporated, but still it persisted. Mrs. Asquith tried again. 'I'll cure Sonia's shyness,' confidently, she told Mamma. 'Just leave her to me.'

Kill or cure. A day or two later she invited me to luncheon at 10 Downing Street where, on arrival in the dining-room, I found my place had been laid between the Prime Minister and Lord Kitchener. The Prime Minister was preoccupied but, politely, he roused himself to ask me a few dates in history which I could not answer. Having promised Mamma I would talk then, with desperate courage, I turned to Lord Kitchener.

Up to that moment, my knowledge of him had been confined to recruiting-posters from which he pointed an enormous finger and glared out searchingly at me over the caption: 'Your Country Needs You!' I knew nothing of his character and, mercifully, was unaware of his aversion to children. Quaveringly, I asked him: 'Have you got a dog?' 'No, I have not!' he snapped back. 'I hate dogs!'

Alas! that I should have been the cause of one of Mrs. Asquith's few failures. Without even attempting to help myself to the next course, scarlet in the face (and nose), I hung my head and dissolved into tears. And when I returned, in disgrace, to Grosvenor Street, I carried a note from Mrs. Asquith to Mamma. 'Don't bring Sonia out, dearest Alice,' she wrote. 'Let her try something else.'

Almost overnight, I discovered Edward Keppel, which was all the more surprising as he had always been there. From early childhood we had featured together in family groups at Quidenham, at one moment with our clothes almost identical:

sailor-hats, starched dresses with sashes, Buster Brown locks. Like small but essential pieces in the same jigsaw puzzle, we had fitted into our allotted places in the family album, but with our individual values to each other hardly recognized. In my early childhood I went more often to Duntreath than to Quidenham and I knew my Edmonstone cousins much better than my Keppel cousins. And then, suddenly, Edward and I met face to face.

At Eton Long Leave, 1915, Mamma took a party of boys and girls to the Hippodrome to see 'Joyland'. It was my first visit to a music hall and I can remember Miss Shirley Kellog and Bertram Wallis singing patriotic songs before draped Union Jacks. A gangway led from the back of the stalls to the stage and down it pranced the chorus girls, trained like cavalry horses in what appeared to be the highest forms of 'dressage'. They passed quite close to our party and the boys grew pink and excited and the girls (including me) felt rather cross and jealous. But, once the chorus was at a safe distance on the stage we all thought it wonderful. Later, we went back home to Grosvenor Street to a buffet-supper and dancing to the gramophone. Then I realized what fun it was to have a male cousin two years older than myself (as good as a brother, and even better). When Edward kissed me 'good night' he said, 'Let's write'.

At that time, Papa's shirt-front was out of reach and I was badly missing him. Although I wrote him regularly, the every-day events and thoughts I had been wont to tell him seemed too trivial to pass through censorship and field post office; also my writing was large and they took up too much room. So I kept them back although they needed saying, as a room needs daily dusting to keep clean. Now, here was Edward, Papa in embryo, with the same straight hair and blue eyes and (thank God!) the same high Keppel nose; and, apparently the same desire to know what I was doing. Even if only temporarily, he seemed heaven-sent to fill Papa's place. So, in reply to his suggestion, delightedly I answered: 'Oh! yes, let's.'

It was Edward who inspired me with an interest in my personal appearance, and who encouraged me secretly to powder my nose to subdue its crimson hue. My cloth-topped boots were to be reserved for winter but he bought me a pair of brown suede shoes for summer, laced with brown ribbon and with Louis Quinze heels. Fortified by his approval, I began to enter a room with more confidence, and when I had got through a visit or two to Eton without mishap, I began to feel I could hold my own with my own generation at least. Hardly a day passed without a letter to each other, loving, laughing, frivolous, like kites of brightly coloured paper streaking irresponsibly through the sky.

Now I visited Quidenham often, and came more and more under the spell of my Keppel relations, with their hooked noses and direct blue eyes. Every member of the family possessed these features, both male and female, and even Aunt Gertie seemed to have acquired them by propinquity. I felt part of Quidenham (which I had never quite done at Duntreath) and very much part of the Keppel family, both in looks and tastes.

Uncle Arnold was a sculptor, an artist (and brilliant caricaturist) and a boat-builder, and could have made a career for himself in any of these trades. In the front hall at Quidenham reclined the life-sized figure of a nude female, in white marble. (Confronted by a model of such obvious allurements, Aunt Gertie had thought it prudent to accompany Uncle Arnold to his London studio where, while he sculpted, alertly she had watched him shape the rough marble into curves.) In the fore-court outside, stood the defiant figures of two drummer-boys cast in bronze, dramatically portraying Kipling's heroes: 'The drums of the Fore and Aft'. And the front door itself was guarded by a row of toy cannon, all modelled by Uncle Arnold's skilful hand.

The interior of Quidenham House enchanted me with its contrasts of grandeur and cosiness, and decorum and ease. Bought in 1762 by my ancestor, General George, 3rd Earl of Albemarle, with the money he had been awarded as Commander-in-Chief of the landing force in the campaign in which he and his brother, Admiral William Augustus Keppel, had jointly effected the capture of Havana earlier that year, each succeeding generation had contributed something to it, sometimes of value, sometimes not, but nearly always preserved in, as I thought, the haphazard manner in which it had been put down. As a boy, Joshua Reynolds had run away to sea under the protection of young Captain Keppel whom thereafter he painted at various stages of his naval career, together with other members of his family. In consequence, at one time, the walls of Quidenham had been lined with family portraits painted by Sir Joshua. By the time I noticed them, some of the originals had passed, by marriage, into other families, and others had had to be sold for cash. But the remainder looked down at me with the same quizzical expression that I saw reflected in the living faces round me.

Uncle Arnold and Aunt Gertie had four sons and one daughter, all radiating facets from the same precious stone. I was told that in childhood they had been brought up very strictly but, by 1915, the strictness could be considerably stretched like good quality elastic which, as far as I was concerned, only snapped back after the front door closed. Even for Edward, nearly always it could be sidetracked by a direct appeal to Uncle Arnold's or Aunt Gertie's sense of humour, from which boundless stream their children's humour flowed.

By the summer of 1915, Uncle Arnold and Aunt Gertie had plenty of anxiety to damp their humour down. Their two elder sons, Bury and Arnold, were in France, on active service; Rupert, already wounded and taken prisoner, had been maliciously singled out to serve a term of solitary confinement; Betty was a V.A.D. in France; and Edward was about to leave Eton for Sandhurst, thereafter to join the Rifle Brigade. Their whole family had been mobilized from the day war started but its martial background had been always such a part of it that they appeared to accept it as inevitable. (Even two of Uncle Arnold's and Papa's sisters, Aunt Theo Davidson and Aunt

Hilda Keppel, were at that moment, also on active service, nursing in France.)

Strangely enough, Uncle Arnold stamped my family sense in me more deeply than ever Papa had done. Papa's family saga had been skilfully told, but on an excitingly fictional basis, belonging to the cinematograph or theatre. Uncle Arnold made me realize that I was part of it. And, as far as he and his brothers and sisters were concerned, once I got to Quidenham he and they had no need to tell me anything further as Quidenham said it all. From childhood up, I read of their lives in the family album. Even in those days, the girls had seemed to play almost an equal part with the boys in their work and pleasures, and both boys and girls had seemed to develop their notably independent spirit at a very early age. In after life, probably Uncle Derek became the most law-abiding member of the family. (As Master of the Royal Household, I suppose he had to be.) But, in childhood, he appeared to differ very little in enterprise from his brothers and sisters, and Uncle Arnold's hair raising reminiscences always included him. Needless to say, I was fascinated by early photographs of Papa. As a boy, he had outgrown his strength (he was known as 'The Wolf' for his cadaverous appearance at school), and, at the age of 19, had been sent out to South Africa for a year, in the care of Cecil Rhodes. Later, he had worked as a lumberjack, in Canada; and in a mining-camp, in Colorado. Already, I knew this, but I had never seen photographs of him doing these things, before. By the time I knew Papa, he had a place in life, and family responsibilities. But in his early manhood he had looked lean and tough and carefree, with a long way to go before he settled down. And what of the Amazons, Papa's sisters? Through the pages of the album they grew up, slim and handsome and alert. Four of them had married, but one of these, Aunt Mary Tagart, had died when I was six. Aunt Hilda had never married; and Aunt Lena had become a nun. In all nine faces I thought I could trace the same characteristics of humour, enterprise, adventure. And each face seemed to display these characteristics independently of sex. Had they been men, I felt that inevitably my aunts too would have been soldiers or sailors. And, even as it was, in after years, Aunt Theo's and Aunt Hilda's war records read almost identically with those of their menfolk: 'Lady Theodora Davidson, D.St.J. Matron of a French Military Hospital in France during World War I, Medaille de la Reconnaissance Française (2 medals); Lady Hilda Keppel, served as a V.A.D. in World War I in France 1915–17 (1915 Star, 2 medals).' Somehow, I got the impression that Admiral Keppel's telescope was being trained on me, with my father and his brothers and sisters watching me, kindly but rather critically, through it, to see which of the Service Units I myself would choose.

Edward took me rabbiting and I forced myself to pick up dead rabbits without flinching. And once he suggested my riding, but I got out of that by not having any suitable clothes. Wherever he went, devotedly I followed him, determined to keep up with him, at last with the proud sense that I belonged to the country and that the soil-ties of Norfolk could legitimately bind me as tightly as they did him. Panting after him, I scratched myself on brambles and stumbled over stubble fields, while every now and then, Edward would shout back at me encouragingly: 'Come on, darling, you're doing very well.'

As the Zeppelins bombed London again in September, with much more resulting damage, I spent the autumn with Rosalind (Lindy) at Buckhurst, working on the land. By then, with German submarines a mounting danger to our food supplies, the Government was laying increasing emphasis on the need to grow more food at home, and Lindy and I (dressed in breeches, thick shoes and stockings and flannel shirts and ties) both felt we were doing valuable war work. We harvested and dug up plots in the kitchen garden, and helped transform some of Cousin Evie's beautiful flower borders into vegetable beds. And, in between times, had a lot of fun.

The life at Buckhurst was unlike any that I had known before, comprising a balance between the arts and athletics which was taken by the various members of the Benson family as a matter of course. Cousin Robin was a scholar, a musician and a painter, and had been an outstanding runner both at Eton and Oxford. His three sons (Guy, Rex and Con) mournfully informed me that at school they had not worked as hard as their father and neither had they run as fast. Yet, even so, all three of them had been in Sixth Form, at Eton, and had won their running Shields. At intervals, during my stay at Buckhurst, they came back on leave, and I fell in love with each one of them in order of seniority. Con and his delightful cousin, Eric, took Lindy and me on paperchases where, treating my asthmatical shortcomings with compassion, sometimes they left me on a hilltop to run literal circles round me. On such occasions, Lindy kept up with them quite easily, running as effortlessly and tirelessly as they.

Guy sang, and Rex and Con played the piano and so did Lindy, who had a love for all forms of music: classical, ballet, jazz. At that time she was studying at the Royal College of Music and, as it seemed to me, could play anything as effortlessly as she ran.

Outside their own family, the Bensons were enthusiastic talent-spotters, often spurring on their guests to unattempted heights. At home, Papa had encouraged me to sing to his accompaniment but this, in the privacy of his sitting-room, not in public. Singing in chorus was a favourite indoor pastime at Buckhurst, and having learnt through this that I could sing quite tunefully, before I knew where I was, I was accorded almost 'prima donna's' honours. Though largely unmerited, applause rang sweetly in my ears as qualifying me to take my place in the Benson circle. Before very long, I was singing solos to Lindy's accompaniment and was being encouraged by Cousin Robin to have my voice trained.

Next to playing the piano, Lindy loved dancing and, on our return to London, Cousin Evie and Mamma succumbed to her entreaties and arranged a class of Russian dancing at Grosvenor Street, with a former member of Diaghilev's Russian Ballet to instruct us. Violet and some of her friends joined us and I can remember Bettine Stuart-Wortley, Clare Tennant (Bim's sister), Cynthia Hamilton and Cimmie Curzon. Clare was the prettiest and Lindy the most graceful pupil. I did better in this class than I had done in Mrs. Wordsworth's but I was no star in this one either. We embarked on hand and feet exercises (these last acutely painful to me in my blocked-toed ballet shoes) and then, owing to the increasing risk of air raids, Cousin Evie and Mamma decided to stop the course. Just galvanized to action, we all sank back into inanition again, like the toys in the 'Boutique Fastasque'.

Imperceptibly at first, Papa's letters were changing. Although nearly always they contained something to laugh at, through them now seemed to ooze a trickle of mud from France. He spent his fiftieth birthday in the trenches and Mamma and I went and chose him a food-hamper at Fortnum & Mason for him to celebrate it with his men. Enthusiastically, he thanked us both and told us that he and his Company had much enjoyed the contents of the hamper but so, unfortunately, had some rats. Would we be sure only to send tinned foods in future? No cardboard box was ratproof, and the birthday cake had especially attracted them.

I was appalled. Fancy rats eating Papa's birthday cake! Although I had no real idea of their horrors, for a second intuition gave me an insight into the misery and filth of the trenches and of the heroic efforts of middle-aged volunteers like Papa, in their struggles to survive.

Violet was working in a canteen for soldiers in Grosvenor Gardens and now I asked Mamma whether I, too, could do some war work. I murmured something about it making me feel better about Papa. Being Mamma, she refrained from saying that I was too young at fifteen to do war work and promised to try to arrange something that did not cut too drastically into my lessons. Largely through Daisy de Brienen's intervention, who was now a driving force in the canteen world, Moiselle and I were shortly afterwards signed on to help at Lady Limerick's Canteen for Soldiers, at London Bridge.

Two innovations heralded our reception there: I was allowed to put up my hair to work there; and Moiselle and I travelled to London Bridge by tube.

I can still remember my first moments of agonized shyness behind the counter; the noise of the station and the rumble of the Underground, making the men's requests inaudible; the boiling, hissing urns of tea and coffee and the piles of white china cups and saucers; the medley of grey-veiled canteen workers bustling round me, giving me instructions I was slow to understand; the piles of sandwiches and buns and tins of fillings and cocoa and coffee; the trays of knives and spoons; the totally inadequate washing-up facilities; and last, but by no means least, the incomprehensible lists I was expected to memorize, at once. Within the narrow orbit of the urn, the air was as hot and damp as in the jungle. But, just outside it, the station draughts stabbed at me with steel-like directness, making me catch my breath. Just for a second, I felt like ducking under the barrier and running away. And then a Tommy asked me for a cup of coffee and a ham sandwich, and I was saved.

Thereafter (and when I had had time to master those awful lists) I came to enjoy the bustle and the sense of urgency transcending it, and to be on my mettle to serve the men quickly. The busy times were the most impersonal. Having mastered the simple technique of it, I used to bawl out the orders to the urn manipulators: 'Fifty teas, twenty coffees, ten cocoas', and then race round balancing as many plates of sandwiches and buns as possible along my arm. When the draft rushes were on it was impossible to distinguish individual faces. I saw a mass of discs in a sea of khaki, topped by tin hats, and framed in heavy kit. There was no time for talk. 'Cup o' tea and a packet o' fags, miss' rang through my ears like a litany. But, between drafts, for the first time, I met men from all over the British Isles and the Dominions; with a smattering of French and Belgian soldiers as well. With my hair up, they treated me as a woman, and showed me photographs of their wives and families as though I had a family of my own. Occasionally, flatteringly, they would ask me: 'Your old man out there?' And, quite truthfully, I would answer, 'Yes, he is.'

Moiselle and I worked at London Bridge Canteen for two years. At the end of it, very unexpectedly, we were given the accolade and presented with the Ribbon of the Order of Queen Elizabeth of the Belgians by a Belgian lady sent over especially to reward British canteen workers for the part they had played in befriending Belgian soldiers during the first two years of war. Neither Moiselle or I dared to claim the medals so, for a long time, the ribbons remained pinned to our pincushions until one day mine, at least, dropped off the pincushion and was swept up with the dust.

Just before Christmas Papa (now a major) came home on leave and his altered appearance gave us all a shock. He had left us with a back as straight as a sword blade. He returned to us with it curved like a scimitar, and this because he was too tall to stand upright in his dugout. (I had a briefly terrifying vision of Guy Fawkes in 'Little Ease'.) Mamma did her best to entertain him. I was allowed to stay up for one or two little dinner-parties for him when his reaction to each of them was the same. He was too tired to compete. Sitting at the head of his table between, as Mamma said, 'the two prettiest women in London', whom ordinarily he would have delighted in, he turned his blue eyes from one to the other and smiled at them while, obviously, his thoughts were far away. Mamma arranged theatre and bridge parties for him, but really he seemed happiest pottering about in his sitting-room, sometimes accompanying me on his piano, but, more often than not, just dropping off to sleep in his green armchair with his hand in mine.

I grew up a lot during Papa's first leave home. A curtain

seemed to drop down behind me, blotting out my childhood, and suddenly the positions were reversed. Now, here was Papa, dependent on me. Still shy to express my sympathy, I sat quietly beside him and, after a while, I could gauge his periods of sleep to a nicety: at first, short periods of five or ten minutes, then, gradually, an hour, or sometimes two. On waking, he liked to find me beside him. Still vulnerable from sleep, then sometimes, I could induce him to talk a little. 'Is it awful, at the Front, Papa?' once I asked him. And he nodded back at me, gravely smiling. 'Not too good, Doey,' he admitted, pressing my hand. 'Not too good.'

A briefly terrible Christmas at Crichel, where tragedy had stalked, unheralded, into that Lucullan scene. Ever since the preceding winter, Gerard Sturt had lain a cripple, paralysed from the waist downwards from the dreadful wounds he had sustained in France. Always, I had preferred Gerard to the rest of his family, partly because he had held himself aloof from Loïs's 'calf-baitings', and partly because he was so romantically good-looking. Of a Pre-Raphaelite beauty, he could have posed as a knight in armour to Burne-Jones. Even in childhood, he had given me the impression that he wanted to escape from his family and, now that he was dependent on it as a cripple, I wondered how he was fitting in.

In the train, on the way down, Papa and Mamma were wondering too. 'I do hope that Humphrey and Feo will make a big effort with poor Gerard this Christmas,' Mamma said.

But, from the moment we all entered the house, it was obvious that the tension between Gerard and his father and mother was strained to snapping point. Everything he did was wrong: he was late for dinner; his chair pulled up the tintacks in the drawing-room carpet; it took up too much room at the dining-room table; difficulties were continually made as to where his nurse had her meals; and because he had asked for his own sitting-room.

The tension persisted throughout Christmas Day and then, at tea-time, Lord Alington stumbled over Gerard's dog and lost his temper. 'You and your dog are nothing but a nuisance in this house,' he raged. White of face, Gerard replied harshly: 'Then, obviously, the solution is for me and my dog to move elsewhere.'

'Which I hope will be to us, in Grosvenor Street,' Mamma put in quickly. 'You can have your own sitting-room and we can put up your nurse.' Without waiting for Gerard to thank her then, briefly but terrifyingly, she reverted to her Olympian status. Looking like Athene, and with her eyes flashing, she turned on Lord Alington. Bitingly she said: 'As for you, Humphrey, you ought to go down on your knees and beg Gerard's pardon. And then pick the rest of the tintacks out of your beastly carpet with your teeth.'

The upshot of it all was that Gerard broke away from his family and came to London, but to the house of a friend of his, Mrs. Julie Thompson, and not to ours.

But, before this, Papa had gone back to the rats and mud in France, in some way oddly fortified by the knowledge of Gerard's helplessness. More than ever, he reminded me of St. Christopher as he kissed me 'good-bye'.

Chapter Eleven

1916

'DRAT THE war!' Nannie exclaimed. 'It's upsetting everybody.' And there were disheartening instances of this, by 1916.

For one thing, disturbingly bad feelings had fomented between the men at the front and the munition-workers, at home. To meet the constant cry for reinforcements a Conscription Bill had been introduced, applied to all men between 18 and 40, but with clauses for exemption in it for those engaged on essential national service. Mamma explained to me that local tribunals granted these exemptions which, sometimes, created bitterness. The same tribunals also could grant exemptions to men who were conscientious objectors to military service. It seemed very sad to think that bad feelings existed between two such vital units of the war effort, but nearly every family had someone fighting for it now and women with sons or husbands at the front were apt to view suspiciously any man in civilian clothes not wearing the qualifying badge of discharge or disablement. Jibes of 'Shirkers!' and 'Conshies!' sometimes were most unfairly made and deplorable incidents occurred when women proffered white feathers to blameless victims. (One of the Grenfell twins, Julian's cousin, was reported to have been given a white feather, on leave, just after he had received the D.S.O.) On the other hand, the munition-workers were frightened by the new law enabling the Government to force unskilled men on them in the factories and perhaps even to subject them to military disci-

MAMMA
painted by Flamingue
1908

MYSELF, BEFORE THE 'UNVEILING'

pline inside the factories. So, in March and April, some of them struck against these measures, on the Clyde. More serious than these, also in April, an armed rebellion broke out in Dublin. This was sternly dealt with and some of the ringleaders, including Sir Roger Casement, the Irish nationalist, were executed. Some of them were incarcerated in the Tower of London and I thought of poor Aunt Louie, nervously averting her eyes from 'Traitor's Gate'. Nevertheless, parallel to all these troubles, our lives went on and, in a way, the routine of war was our safeguard. Once accustomed to it, it toughened our resistance to new alarms.

The Zeppelin raids became more frequent and, again, I was sent off for a week or two, to farm at Buckhurst. But my sixteenth birthday was to be spent in London and, this time, I greatly looked forward to the little party Mamma had promised me, at home.

Mamma now had a contact between the English and French hospitals which occasionally took her to Paris. While there, she bought me a dress from a new shop, Jeanne Lanvin, which catered for young girls' clothes. It was made of royal blue tulle and was modestly 'décolleté'; the skirt was flounced, and the sleeves and hem were edged with skunk. Admittedly, the skunk smelt powerfully but I did not mind. It was my first almost 'grown-up' party-dress, and I thought it beautiful.

Early in May, Papa wrote that his battalion had been engaged in a 'little battle'. Beyond saying that the battalion had behaved magnificently, he made light of it, but he added 'Bobby (White) was on leave, so I was in command'. As a result, a few days later he wrote to say that he hoped to get some leave towards the end of May. So then, of course, my party was postponed until he came.

I can still remember my excitement at the thought of it. There were to be about twenty-five couples, enough to justify the use of Papa's invitation-book. Pandering to my ego, Mamma allowed me to send out invitations: 'Mrs. Keppel—At Home—May 31st, 1916—Dancing—9.30.' I felt I owed it

10

to Papa to keep his book meticulously and all the headings were written in red ink with elaborate rulings underneath. There were practically no entries in the columns headed: 'Old Men' and 'Ladies'. Edward (now commissioned to the Rifle Brigade) headed the list of 'Young Men' and all my girl-friends were alphabetically listed under 'Girls'. Through Edward and some of my girl-friends (notably Teddy Leon) there were to be a good number of young men, as long as their military or naval duties did not interfere with their attendance. And I was rather coyly anticipating a delightful evening as, lately, I had met a particularly nice young man in the Welsh Guards, called Billy, who had assured me that he would do everything possible to attend. There was to be a band (a pianist and a drummer), and a buffet-supper left to Perriat's ingenuity to prepare. Nobody drank much at the parties I had so far attended, but there was to be some white wine cup for those who wanted to.

When Papa returned home, he was in much better spirits and confided to me that he had been thrilled to command the battalion during the battle. Everyone had been splendid, officers and men alike, and it had all gone according to plan.

Innocently, I asked him, 'Will you get a medal for it?' And Papa looked as embarrassed as a schoolboy as he answered: 'I shouldn't think so.'

This time we went to lots of plays together: 'Bric a Brac'; 'The Bing Boys'; 'A Kiss for Cinderella'. Tacitly, we chose plays that made us laugh and musical comedies or 'revues', where we could sing the choruses, and where Papa could spot the chorus-girl with the best legs. (I suppose that Mamma and Violet sometimes accompanied us but, if so, my selfish memory has effaced them.)

The evening of the party arrived, and I felt sick with excitement and, also, terribly hot. Mamma had had my hair waved and it hung down thickly, covering my shoulders like a postilion's cape. Despite my precautionary dabs of powder, beads of perspiration showed on my forehead and I was quite relieved when Mamma decreed that I should encase my clammy hands in gloves. The smell of skunk persisted above its sousing of 'Rose Geranium' but Papa (who had a broken nose) said that I smelt delicious.

As the evening wore on, unaccountably a feeling of uneasiness generated through the ballroom. On the landing outside, the small knot of Mamma's and Papa's friends came and went and, after a while, there seemed to be a continuous stream of people on the stairs. The band was excellent and the supper was lovely but, again and again, the eyes of those of us who were dancing returned to watch the serious faces on the landing. Then Mamma went across and spoke to the pianist, and the music stopped. 'There's been a battle,' she said, 'a naval battle. And it's still going on. As we don't yet know the result of it, I don't think you can go on dancing. So I've asked the band to play the National Anthem, and then I'm afraid I must ask you all to go.'

One by one our guests shook hands with Mamma, thanked her and departed while, miserably, I watched them. Then, apprehensively, I asked her: 'When shall we know about this battle?'

'Probably tomorrow,' soberly, she answered.

But, by the next day, there was nothing definite and there are still people to argue as to whether the Battle of Jutland was a victory for the British Navy, or a draw.

My loyalties have always inclined towards individuals rather than to causes, and sudden sunshine pierced the sombre scene for me when, in June, I knew that Papa was to return from France to command a composite battalion of the East Lancashire Regiment, in Ireland. Although I realized that the war situation was still perilous and that our defence of Verdun appeared to be unending, with Papa within safe distance again selfishly I felt that I could push it out of focus. (Momentarily, I was shocked when poor Lord Kitchener's ship was torpedoed on its way to Russia, and he was drowned. But, later, I am afraid I made full and callous use of my brief acquaintanceship with him, when recounting the occasion of it, at Miss Wolff's.) It meant very little to me that Papa seemed distressed at having to leave his present battalion. 'Who wants a cushy job, at a time like this?' he said. All I knew was that, with him at home again, I could relax and shake myself free from the continual sense of oppression which had enveloped me all the time he was in France.

I hope that his family's undisguised delight at having him back helped him to tolerate the 'know-alls' who now gathered round him to tell him how the war was going. Within a day of his return they were at him (friends and acquaintances who had got no nearer to the war than to read an occasional war map, at their clubs). They took pains to explain the whole strategic plan to him. ('In France, my dear George, you only saw a little bit of the fighting.' 'In your section probably you never realized that the main offensive was at——'.) Like mosquitoes, they buzzed round him, stinging here and there, and, to Papa, mosquito-bites were poisonous. Even Mamma stung him sometimes: 'Well, after all, Georgie darling, Winston told me so.' The poison dispersed quickly but it made Papa irritable, especially when the mosquitoes concerted together to insinuate that his own first-hand war news was no longer up-to-date. They seemed to take a lively pleasure in doing this, as though to get even with him for playing a militant part they had had no heart for. Inevitably, Papa sought out Uncle Arnold for comfort, taking me with him, and then I realized how effectively one brother balanced the other; were one to be momentarily weakened from outside, the other put his shoulder to that weakness and bolstered it up again.

Luckily for him, in a few days Papa left for Ireland to take up his command outside the Curragh. His initial introduction seemed to go off well, and he was settling down quite happily when the news came to him that his beloved 10th Royal Fusilier Battalion had been virtually wiped out at the Battle

of Pozieres (at the outset of the Somme offensive), and that all
the officers had been killed or wounded, with two exceptions,
Colonel Bobby White and his Second-in-Command, Major
Dallas-Waters. Papa's letters became distracted. 'I'd go back
as a subaltern again, if they would have me,' he wrote to
Mamma. 'And to think I was sitting fatly here, on my fanny,
while they were tearing their guts out, over there!'

Tears of sympathy filled Mamma's eyes as she read his
letters: 'Poor darling Papa! He'll never get over missing the
"big" battle,' she said.

In August, Papa and his new battalion went into camp in
Connemara, and Papa wrote that he had found a house to
accommodate us all, and would we please come. He admitted
that it would be a tight squeeze but, given good weather, he
was sure we would like it. And it was nice and near the camp,
he added, so that By and Do could get some riding.

If Violet and I felt qualms about the last part of his letter
we concealed them from each other. Mamma sent us off to
Swears & Wells to buy some riding clothes (Violet, a riding-
habit; me, some breeches). Sitting erect on the girth section
of a wooden horse, we both felt confident. Both of us were
equipped with bowler-hats, and covert coats, and thong-less
whips but, as neither of us possessed boots, we had to make do
with shooting-stockings. It was only when we saw the amusement expressed on the Irish faces round us that we began to
wonder if we looked all right. None of the local population
were as smart as we were but most of them rode and, somehow,
they looked more genuine. Admittedly, we only had the Army
remounts to ride but I doubt if we would have looked better
on anything more spirited. Luckily, usually Papa and Mamma
were blind to defects in their family so, to them at least, we
cut fine figures.

The accommodation in the house certainly was limited and
Rolfe and Perriat slept in a tent in the garden. The garden was
much drier than the house, where Rolfe complained that the
silver was permanently tarnished. As it was war-time, we

had had to restrict our importation into Ireland of china and glass and linen but, even so, our arrival created quite a stir. After a while, Aunt Ida and Uncle Archie arrived to stay, each with a maid and valet, and they and Nannie and Miss Williams provided a retinue seldom before seen in Connemara. With other guests besides, daily we sallied from the house like sight-seeing foreigners (which, indeed, we were). Of all the company, undoubtedly, Perriat and I enjoyed ourselves the most. (Perriat became almost uncontrollably Swiss and wanted to milk every cow and goat he saw.)

The close proximity of the camp accounted for much of my enjoyment but no one else seemed much to appreciate it. 'Reveille' roused us in the mornings; 'Roll-Call' introduced our nights. In between times, bugles whetted our appetites for meals. Uncle Archie's ears were permanently stuffed with cotton-wool; Mamma and Violet took to sleeping pills. Mamma tried to get Papa to do away with 'Reveille' or, at least, to put it back an hour. But he resisted. 'There's a war on, Freddie darling,' he told her, smiling. 'And I'm not here to train the men to lie in bed.'

Funnily enough, of all the party, Aunt Ida was the most adaptable. That is to say, she continued to live her own life quietly inside the other. Always she was irreproachably punctual for breakfast; luncheon; tea; dinner. She wrote her letters in the morning, in a huge, childish hand, and went for a little walk (wet or fine) before luncheon. In the afternoon, she skimmed through the papers; embroidered a little; went out; came in; had tea. After tea, she embroidered steadily till dressing-time and then again after dinner until the clock struck ten, when she got up, kissed us all and went to bed. By ten o'clock the oil lamps were spluttering wildly and Uncle Archie had more than once observed: 'Ida dear, you'll strain your eyes.' She had to bend perilously near the lamp to control her stitches yet the flame held back, as though itself harnessed to her routine.

For me, the days passed pleasantly enough, running into

September. Then, on September 16th, the thunderbolt fell. Just before tea-time, a telegraph boy arrived, on a bicycle. In his hand he bore a War Office telegram, informing Uncle Archie that his eldest son, Willie, had been killed in battle, on the Somme.

The effect on poor Uncle Archie was appalling. He retired to bed, in a darkened room, and turned his face to the wall, refusing comfort. In vain Mamma entreated him to have some tea, or brandy, or to let her sit beside him. Usually so calm, in her own way and through him, she was almost as distracted as he. Violet (who had been a great friend of Willie's) was equally distressed; I was very sorry but, guiltily, could not produce the depths of sorrow that they did; Papa was at the camp, but had been sent for; and suddenly I realized that no one had given a thought to Aunt Ida since the news had been broken to her, an hour before.

Rapidly, I made a calculation. Ten minutes past six: she must be embroidering. With much more ease than I would have approached Uncle Archie, I went into the sitting-room and shut the door.

Aunt Ida was sitting by the lamp which she seemed to have turned up higher than usual. She was engaged on a bright pattern in greens and yellows and blues. As I came into the room, she was threading a needle with the blue silk and her hand was perfectly steady. As I watched her, suddenly I wanted to cry. 'Aunt Ida,' gruffly, I began, and she put down her work and took my hand in hers.

We sat there, hand-in-hand, in silence, bound by a sympathy beyond the need for speech. Then we heard Mamma's and Papa's voices in the passage, approaching the sitting-room. We heard Mamma saying brokenly: 'Poor Archie! Poor, darling Archie!' Then, in a voice of relief: 'Luckily, dear Ida doesn't feel things like Archie.'

I gave Aunt Ida a horrified look and she returned it quietly. As Mamma and Papa entered the room, she held up her blue silk again.

Which of the graces did the colour blue symbolize, I wondered? Was it Hope? Or Faith?

It was pitch dark on Dunfermline Station platform and it appeared to be deserted, except for Nannie and myself. Between us was our luggage; my trunk, Nannie's suitcase. Although still my loved companion, Julie had been left behind on this occasion, and now I carried my dressing-case in one hand and my bag in the other. To make matters worse it was bitterly cold and raining, a drizzling, icy rain that might easily turn to snow.

'Cousin Freddie *must* have sent to fetch us,' hopefully I said to Nannie. 'As he's Commander-in-Chief, probably there's a car driven by a marine, waiting for us.' To which Nannie replied severely 'Ssh! Remember the train notices ("Walls have ears"). I hope *someone's* fetching us soon, or we'll catch our deaths.'

A shadowy shape approached us, that of the very youthful porter who had taken out our luggage. 'Have ye no' someone to meet ye?' he asked solicitously. 'There'll no' be anither train in the nicht, and I'm awa' hame the noo.'

'Oh! please don't leave us here!' I implored him. 'We're meant to be going to stay at Admiralty House, but they seem to have forgotten to meet us. And,' tearfully, I added: 'If we spend the night on the platform, probably we'll die of cold!'

The porter appeared to be kind-hearted. He was silent a minute, thinking. Then he announced that he himself would drive us to Admiralty House, in his father's farm-cart. This boasted a high driver's seat into which he and I pushed and pulled Nannie. I settled myself in the middle of it; and the porter climbed up last.

From the muffled wagon-lamps, a cautious beam of light shone down on to the carthorse's broad back and, from my point of vantage, his ears pointed forwards and backwards reassuringly as though passing me back messages of comfort. The 'clip-clop' of his iron-shod hooves on the road was the only sound that broke the stillness. Thawing slightly, but still very cold, we all three remained mute.

Then the porter broke the silence. 'Still cauld?' he whispered in my ear, and put an arm round my waist.

Furtively, I looked at Nannie but only a portion of her face was visible above her black fox fur. I had an idea she was asleep. 'Rather cold,' I whispered back, and he squeezed my waist encouragingly. The warmth of his body was most welcome and I leant against it gratefully.

If he did not actually kiss me he came pretty near to it and it would have seemed perfectly natural if he had. Perched up beside him, he and I seemed to develop a bond of warm, glowing youth, in antithesis to the cold, foggy night and the old woman sitting beside us. It wrapped us both round like a cloak, and the warmth it generated showed in our cheeks. Although nameless, I began to feel that I had known the porter for years and that, in some strange way, our future lives were bound up together. I think he felt this too as his grip on me was becoming a clinch. I dared not openly look at him but, under the brim of my hat, I could see the firm outline of his chin and a faintly developed Adam's apple. From his coat emanated the homely smell I had hitherto associated with Dingwall and Mr. Angus, with an extra salty tang to it, like seaweed. His arm pressed my side so tightly that I could hardly breathe and, with sudden alarm, I wondered if I was going to have an attack of asthma. Really, that would spoil things! To counter it, I breathed in and out slowly, as the German doctor had taught me to do.

Suddenly, we turned in through some gates guarded by sentries and drew up, with a flourish, to the back door of Admiralty House. Nannie awoke with a grunt and the romantic stillness was broken by approaching voices. With acute embarrassment, I asked the porter the price of our ride and was further embarrassed by his answer. 'Och! that's all richt!' he said, and would not accept a penny. I felt that there must be some suitable expression of farewell to round off our evening, but I could not think of one. So I thanked him rather lamely, and jumped to the ground. The next moment, my cousins, Jones and Sambo Hamilton, ran out from the house to greet me and, while they were doing so, the porter drove off. I had a brief glimpse of his erect back before his cart passed through the gateway, then his horse's hooves faded away in the distance, and he was gone. 'I'm afraid the car was late meeting you," Jones said apologetically. 'But how on earth did you find a farm-cart to bring you here? And *why* to the back door?' I felt rather shy, when answering her questions, and strangely reluctant to talk about the porter. It was beyond my powers to establish him in her mind as the 'Preux Chevalier' I felt he was.

Romantically begun, my visit to Admiralty House, Rosyth, continued in the same vein. When I looked out of my window next morning, before me I saw displayed some of the scarred survivors of the recent Battle of Jutland: The wounded *Lion*; H.M.S. *Barham*; H.M.S. *Warspite*; H.M.S. *Tiger* and *Indefatigable*. Later, some of their officers came on shore and my susceptibilities reeled from one devastating sailor to another: Sir David Beatty; Admiral Pakenham; glamorous Captains and Commanders; Lieutenant Commanders; Lieutenants; Sub-Lieutenants; Midshipmen. Irrespective of rank, they teased and flirted with me and I took my toll from them in signed photographs. Sir David and Admiral Pakenham made special expeditions into Edinburgh to be photographed and, obviously, in wet weather, as they both wore mackintoshes. There were few women to beguile that crowd of men, and Jones and Sambo and I were treated as enchantresses. Sometimes, my curtains parted to reveal an empty harbour; the Fleet had stolen out overnight on some secret exercise. On such occasions, the war came dramatically back to us again and, rather guiltily, we resumed our sober occupations, knitting jerseys and seaboot stockings. But when the Fleet was in we were 'en fête', with every serious thought banished except the desire to please. Some of the younger sailors became my lasting friends: Turtle and Harry Hamilton (Jones's and Sambo's brothers); Leicester Curzon-Howe; Tommy Fox-Pitt. Beneath all their banter I sensed the validity of their friendships and, ecstatically, I felt like Penelope welcoming back Ulysses.

The time came for me to leave and a little pang shot through my heart as I reached Dunfermline Station. Although I had barely given him a thought since the night of my arrival, I was disappointed not to find the young porter on the platform. Instead, an aged man with whiskers heaved our luggage into the train.

It was several weeks after my return home that I received a letter:

'Dear Miss,' it read, 'I got your name and address from a marine at Admiralty House, and thought you would like to know that I've joined the Army. I hope to go back to my job as a porter after the war, and then I should be able to support a wife. Please write and send me a snapshot. Hoping this finds you as it leaves me. XXXXXXX

Your loving Johnnie McPhail
Private No. ......
Unit ......'

In great excitement, I ran with the letter to Mamma who, to my distress, forbade me to answer it. 'You know you don't really want to be a porter's wife, Doey,' realistically she said.

Reluctantly, I had to admit the force of her argument—it was always reasonable—and agreed to tear up the letter. But my feeling of regret persisted, as I dropped the small pieces into the waste-paper basket. It seemed such a pity to ignore a firm offer.

We were all getting a bit hungry by November 1916, and a lot of people felt that the Government ought to bring in compulsory rationing. People in the country were better off than those in the towns and the distribution of food was not always equal. Appeals for food economy had not got far. (In Grosvenor Street, Mamma had pooled the meals above and below stairs. The schoolroom meals had been done away with, and the inmates of 'the Room' and 'the Hall' now ate, rather reluctantly, together.) As I was overgrown and thin, Mamma had got me a doctor's order for more milk, but butter was universally scarce and we largely depended on an occasional gift of it from Lady Ilchester or Cousin Evie. The outcry against the general shortage became so acute that a special Food Controller was appointed but, with the submarine menace growing daily more serious, he had little he could control, poor man. The dreadful alternatives of 'Guns or Butter' weighed in the balance and the Government was becoming the whipping-boy for everybody's grievances. Some of its members had already been accused of pro-German sympathies. Despite the fact that, as War Minister, he had done more than anyone to reorganize the Army at the outbreak of hostilities, Violet's friend, Lord Haldane, had had to resign already, largely because he had gone to school in Germany. (If that went for Lord Haldane, what about Violet and me?) And poor Mr. Asquith himself was accused of being too lenient to German prisoners. (When Moiselle heard this she remained out of reach of his handshake whenever he came to Grosvenor Street, and distantly bowed her head.) There were general complaints that too many shirkers evaded 'Call-up', and that the Government were not forceful enough to achieve full effort. All these complaints came back to Mr. Asquith and in December, he resigned.

The implications of his resignation were immediately felt at 16 Grosvenor Street as, homeless from 10 Downing Street, he and his family came there. Mamma moved out of her own bedroom for Mrs. Asquith, and moved into Papa's room; Mr. Asquith went into the spare room; and their son, Anthony, (aged fourteen) was accommodated in a vacant maid's room. (Their daughter, Elizabeth, went to some other friends.)

Most of Mrs. Asquith's tremendous correspondence was maintained at night, and for this ordeal she asked to be fortified with sandwiches. These she would pick at and frequently forget to consume. But even so, they meant butter, and butter was scarce.

Eventually, Fortnum & Mason solved the problem with some sort of composite filling which Mrs. Asquith absorbed quite happily. Neither Mr. Asquith nor Anthony (Puffin) made any nocturnal demands on Mamma's kitchen. In the day-time, Mr. Asquith looked tired and ill and probably had not slept much, but he made great conversational efforts, and so did Puffin. (Puffin had the best manners of any schoolboy I had met.) Mrs. Asquith was outspoken against her husband's critics but about them he was silent. He seemed to have lost interest in the present and to have slipped back into the past.

Chapter Twelve

1917

ON JANUARY 1st, 1917, Edward was gazetted to the
2nd Battalion Rifle Brigade and on January 25th he
left England to join it, in France.

He had left Sheerness just before Christmas, as a qualified
Brigade Instructor in Bombing and, by the time he came to say
good-bye, he seemed to me to have become an experienced
soldier. Latterly, I had not seen quite so much of him as
formerly and the two-year gap of age between us seemed to
have widened. On January 12th I had been to his 'thé-dansant'
(to celebrate his nineteenth birthday) and, guiltily, I knew that
I had not much enjoyed it. Edward had been surrounded
by pretty girls of his own age and I had felt very young and
gawky.

As always, he had included me in everything, but the talk
had been mainly of parties he and his friends had been to in the
evenings to which I was too young to be invited. And two
particularly pretty girls had been present, Avie Sackville and
Jean Kinloch. A wave of jealousy had surged over me as I
looked at them, followed by an abject sense of envy. How
could I hope to compete with such sparkling eyes, such curly
hair, such tiny *retroussé* noses? Stoutly, I had proclaimed my
enjoyment of the 'thé-dansant' (the first I had been to) but, by
the time Moiselle had arrived to fetch me I had been glad to
leave.

When Edward came to say good-bye, he gave me a 'précis'

of nearly all he had done and was going to do for the rest of his embarkation-leave, taking it for granted that I would enjoy the hearing of it as much as he did the telling. As always, I was flattered by his confidences, but my new feeling of jealousy blunted my pleasure a little. I took care to disguise it and our meeting seemed as gay as usual until the moment came for him to go. Then the full import of my approaching separation from him and my fears for his safety broke on me. It was as though I was saying good-bye to Papa again, but to a Papa miraculously rejuvenated. This one was my own contemporary, almost interchangeable with myself, and with a shared present and future.

With no disloyalty to Papa in my heart, I realized that the ties of relationship now between Edward and myself were different and, in a sense, more poignant. Where I had first loved Edward because he had so resembled Papa, now it seemed to me that I had grown to love him partly because, in some idealized way, he stood as an embodiment of myself, as I would have been had I been Papa's son. (He had all the qualities that Papa loved, integrity, courage, humour, all of which Papa had sought to inculcate in me from childhood up, and in which frequently I had failed, because I was a girl.) And partly, now I knew I loved him because he had made me dependent on him, building me up, even to myself, and presenting me, in better shape, to the world, as a youthful Svengali might have presented a still more youthful Trilby. I did not suppose that consciously he had done so. My dependence on him had emanated from his sympathy. I realized that there was a terribly selfish element about my distress at his going. I would miss him with all my heart, not only because I was losing a loved companion, but because, without his strength, I would lapse back into weakness.

Together, Edward and I went to say 'good-bye' to Nannie, and then I accompanied him down the stairs. In the hall for a moment we clung together, like two lost children. I was glad to have this last moment alone with him. I let him out into the black unlighted street and he saluted me smartly. 'Promise to write to me once a week,' he said.

'Promise,' I answered, as gaily as I could, and managed to smile.

Now there were drastic economies in food, fuel and lighting. Restaurant meals were very much cut down; wine was largely given up. (King George had given up drinking wine for over a year, an example which some of his subjects had been slow to follow.) Due to the increasing air-raids, now London (and apparently other big towns as well) had total black-out. Once the last glimmer of daylight faded from the streets, pedestrians had to depend on the cautious flicker of their torches.

Nevertheless, there was plenty of gaiety behind closed doors and, for me, much of it was associated with Lindy's new dancing-class at 16 South Street. This one took a different form to Russian ballet, and now we gyrated sedately round in a 'Pavane' or 'Minuet', rehearsing for our first charity matinee performance, in aid of the Hospital for Limbless Soldiers at Roehampton.

Being shorter, Lindy and Marjorie Jessel were cast as females; Betty Crawford and I were cast as men. I rather enjoyed my change of sex and seemed to lose much of my shyness when I put on breeches. Probably, therefore I rightly earned Marjorie's teasing criticism: 'What an awful bounder you'd be, if you were a man!'

On the day itself, the 'girls' were arrayed as Court ladies of the eighteenth century, in orthodox full brocaded skirts and tightly fitting bodices; the 'men' were togged up as Court dandies, in satin coats and breeches, beflowered waistcoats and lace ruffles. (To emphasize their manhood, they carried swords as well.)

Two of us wore wigs and two had powdered hair, and all of us were professionally made-up with blackened eye-lashes and greasepaint. We were nervous but enjoying ourselves. To faces unused to powder or mascara the 'maquillage' gave a sudden bloom and we were all conscious of the fact that we looked prettier than usual. (Me, particularly, as my nose looked comparatively small, now that I was disguised as a man.) I think we got through the steps without mishap and took our calls before the curtain afterwards with new-born confidence.

Still unchanged, then I accompanied Lindy back to supper in South Street where, to my delight, I found Con home on leave.

Half-way through supper the maroons started, warning us that an air-raid was probably due over London. Usually, there was an interval of about a quarter of an hour between the warning and the raid, which gave me time to return on foot to Grosvenor Street.

With Con as escort, briskly I started home, up South Audley Street, across one side of Grosvenor Square, to the top of Grosvenor Street. The night was clear (too clear for safety) and we had hardly need of our torches. With only a few more yards for me to go, Con bade me 'good night' and turned for home.

Slightly impeded by my sword clanking against my knees, I proceeded alone down the deserted street, then round the corner from Davies Street, a woman approached me, with her head down. She nearly cannoned into me, before she looked up. When she did so, her jaw dropped, and she let out a scream which must have frozen the blood in the veins of anyone within hearing. 'God preserve us!' she shrieked. 'The ghost of Grosvenor Square!'

It had the most extraordinary effect on me, this implication that I had changed from substance into ether, and it hardly seemed worth the trouble to stand aside to let her pass. Even after she had disappeared, I continued homewards with a lightheaded feeling that my feet were no longer touching the pavement. And when I heard distant bombs dropping their message of danger passed me by. Should I bother to ring the bell, when I reached home, I wondered? Or should I just ooze myself through the key-hole, like laughing-gas?

Abruptly my actions were decided for me. Apparently Rolfe had been watching out for me as, when I approached the front door, it opened and he grabbed me inside. Behind him was Mamma, flatteringly agitated. 'Doey *darling*! Where *have* you been?' she cried. 'You might have been caught in the air-raid!'

It was comforting to be assured that I was still in the land of the living and not just the ghost of a bygone age. And suddenly I was very frightened of the air-raid and more than willing to shelter downstairs.

The implications of the war were getting beyond me and now I depended on Mamma's immediate entourage to interpret its tones and overtones. Things seemed brightest when Sir John Cowans was present, hopefully commenting on the growing magnitude of the German withdrawal to the Hindenburg Line and of the moral effect on the Allies of their capture of Vimy Ridge. Otherwise, her friends took a sombre view. The submarine menace seemed to be getting worse, instead of better, and even the lives of my own friends living in the country now seemed to be singled out for stricture. (Foxhunting recently had been abandoned.) What was far worse, the troops on active service seemed not to be getting proper rations. (In April, Edward wrote a pathetic letter to Aunt Gertie, asking whether she could send him out fresh butter, as he had had bad dysentery due to his unchanging diet of canned food in the trenches.) Voluntary rationing at home again was called for and, once more, Perriat's ingenuity had to devise a way of cutting down.

Then things looked up. The Admiralty introduced the Q-ship into the Navy and with its institution our anti-submarine campaign began; the United States declared war on Germany from which announcement even Mamma's most dubious friends took heart, realizing that large reinforcements

were on their way at last, although they would still take many
months to come.

During all this time I kept up my weekly correspondence
with Edward; and not with Edward only. Almost with the
same sense of dedication as that with which I had undertaken
the composition of my two novels for Volly, I wrote weekly
to Sir David Beatty; Admiral Pakenham; Turtle and Harry
Hamilton; Leicester Curzon-Howe; Tommy Fox-Pitt and
his Welsh Guards brother, Billy; Con Benson; Charlie
Edmonstone; Eddie Edmonstone; another cousin, Eddie
Boyd; Mr. Angus; and Harry Stavordale. Some of my letters
were repetitive of others and these were easy. But others had
to be written for particular persons. (Obviously, the same
range of subjects could not be applied to Sir David Beatty,
on the high seas, as to Harry Stavordale, at Eton, or to Mr.
Angus, farming down in Dorset.) It was not so much vanity
that prompted this prodigious correspondence as a sense of
duty and, as such, it mattered little to me if the contents of
my letters bored the recipients. Together with my Canteen
work and my spasmodic agricultural labours, considering the
seriousness of the war, it was all part of my war-effort and, as
such, painstakingly undertaken to bolster up morale.
Gratifyingly, it produced acknowledgements, not least from
Sir David and Admiral Pakenham who usually wrote politely
hoping to hear from me again. And, in their replies, some of
my younger correspondents appeared grateful and others
flirtatious, and these letters I had to watch carefully, for fear
they would fall into someone else's hands.

Best of all, I loved getting Edward's letters which, whatever
his mood, continued to give me that sense of duality, of simultaneous flowering on the same branch. Sometimes I took them
to show Aunt Gertie, who would confirm this sense. 'Really,
you are ridiculously like Edward!' she would exclaim. 'In the
way you walk, and in the things you say.' And she would read
me some of his letters and we would laugh together at the
funny parts, and worry over his health. In one letter he thanked

her for some wire-cutters: 'As regard the wire-cutters, may I never be called upon to use them in anger! Only people who get V.C.s ever cut wire, and then it's generally a posthumous grant!!!'

In July, Edward came back on leave and again the disparity in our ages divided us. But he went out of his way to stress what fun we would have together in a year's time when he could chaperon me to parties. 'It'll be such a relief to Aunt Alice,' he said, 'not to have to do it herself.' Before he went back, Aunt Gertie and Uncle Arnold gave a dance for him, preceded by a dinner-party at Claridge's. And, again, I was told all about it and saw the letter of thanks he wrote her, afterwards. 'I shall never forget my first leave, and I only hope the next one will be as nice. Give my love to all my friends. Very much au revoir . . .' Two days after writing it he was killed, at the third Battle of Ypres.

My defence was to bottle up my feelings and, if possible, to disguise the fact that I had any. No tears came, when Mamma told me the news. I just said: 'Oh! I see,' and hardly paused in what I was doing. Mamma was nonplussed and even a little shocked, and Papa achieved little more. My dread was that she and he would break through the bastion of my self-control and then I would drown. I wrote to Aunt Gertie and Uncle Arnold and got back wonderful letters of faith, the sort of letters I knew they would write even though their hearts were breaking. But I could do nothing. I had been confirmed earlier in the year and had taken my first Communion seriously. But, for the moment, I recoiled from taking it again as I had nothing to ask God for.

Edward's obituary notices and the letters Uncle Arnold got from his Commanding Officer and some of his men were wonderful but, even so, they could not gloss over the horror of his death. He had been killed leading his men in a counterattack which, alas! had been unsuccessful. The ground over which he had fought had been recaptured, and his body had had to be left unburied. For five months Uncle Arnold and

Aunt Gertie did not know where he lay. His battalion had suffered terrible casualties during the same battle and nearly all its officers were killed or wounded. Eventually, it was relieved by the 2nd Australian Pioneer Battalion and, shortly afterwards, the Commanding Officer wrote Uncle Arnold that Edward's body had been found. He confirmed its burial on December 19th, 1917.

During those five months Uncle Arnold and Aunt Gertie continued to live their lives quite cheerfully, with one son still at the front, another badly wounded and a third still a prisoner of war. In the same way that his ancestors had done before him, stoically Uncle Arnold interpreted his family motto: 'Do not yield to misfortunes'. When Papa told me that I felt ashamed of my own paralysing emotions and decided to carry a secret banner for Edward into the future, as he would have done for me.

Ten years later, I was standing talking to Aunt Gertie beside her writing-table at Quidenham. The sun was setting on a brilliant autumn day and a shaft of its light shone across the floor. Suddenly she said to me: 'Do you know, darling, that twice lately I have seen Edward standing where you are? He just stood there, smiling, without saying anything.' It was an extraordinary remark for her to make but I felt sure she made it with conviction.

A sense of shared happiness went through me, as though Edward and I were standing on the same spot together. Through the window I could see the copse we used to beat through when he was seventeen years old and I, fifteen. I remembered that wherever he had led I had followed, with the same eagerness that I felt his men must have displayed stumbling after him during that last dreadful battle. (Probably he had rallied them with a variant of his call to me: 'Come on, chaps, you're doing splendidly!') And I remembered how proud I had been, those ten long years ago, to feel bound, like him, to Norfolk. (If I felt the strength of soil ties, how much

more strongly must he?) His whole manner of life at Quidenham had proclaimed his love of it. And in almost every letter
home he had extolled it.

Turning my head, I too smiled at Aunt Gertie. 'I'm only
surprised that you haven't seen Edward long before this,' I
said.

Chapter Thirteen

MARCHING TO A STANDSTILL

PERSEVERINGLY, I MADE conversation, peering
at my partner through the candle-lit obscurity of Lady
Lovelace's ballroom. 'I'm afraid it's going to be more and
more difficult to give dances this winter,' ponderously, I said,
'with electricity cut down and so little coal.'

To my embarrassment, he leered knowingly back at me.
'Dances as we know them, Miss Keppel, require neither light
nor warmth!'

I could not afford to snub him, so I tried again. 'Do you ever
find time to go to the cinema in the afternoon?'

'Not by myself, I don't,' he answered me emphatically.
'Going alone to the cinema is a waste of good dark.'

Out of the corner of my eye I saw someone else approaching. Surely it was to invite me to dance. Eagerly I turned,
only to discover that the newcomer was my partner's brother.
'I claim the elder brother's privilege!' gallantly, he said.

On the spur of the moment, I could not make up my mind
which brother was the worse, but anyone was better than no
one so, I took on the elder.

A few weeks before I had gone to my first dance, given by
Lady Winifred Renshaw, in Portman Square. As an appetizer,
first I had been invited to dine with my chaperon, Lady
Kinloch (the mother of Edward's beautiful girl-friend, Jean).

In defiance of Mrs. Asquith's injunctions to the contrary,
Mamma had decided to bring me out after New Year 1918,
but, from the first, she had made it plain that she intended to

chaperon me by delegation only. Not for her was the chaperones' bench; the whispered criticism; the packed descent to the buffet. She painted me a picture of these impossible situations so vividly that argument was useless. 'But, of course, I'll see that *someone* chaperons you to each dance, darling,' she reassured me.

Whether or not it was a psychological reaction to putting up my hair (with the spurious courage any form of disguise seemed to induce in me), up to the actual moment of that first dinner-party I had felt almost confident. Scrupulously I had first observed the trends of fashion and then had prevailed on Mamma to submit to them. Possibly (if rather ambiguously) inspired by loyalty to the troops, across the left shoulder of my pale green dress was slung a 'Sam Browne' belt of velvet acorns, interspersed with holly. A wreath of acorns crowned my hair which was waved with tongs and trained into two side-curls (known as 'chaps') practically across my face. Rouge and lipsalve were not used by débutantes in 1918, but fashion decreed a universally white powdered nose to which I eagerly subscribed, reducing my own prominent organ to a leprous hue. My feet were encased in gold sandals with Bacchanalian ribbons up my legs. And Mamma had fitted me out with elbow-length white gloves. Attired in the trimmings of the moment, almost complacently I had bidden Moiselle farewell in Lady Kinloch's hall and then had given the butler my name, before entering my hostess's drawing-room.

At first sight, all seemed well. The lovely Jean had been present, wearing a becoming variant of my uniform: a yellow chiffon dress with a mimosa 'Sam Browne'; no wreath, but the same conspicuous 'chaps'; green sandalled shoes; no gloves; her delightfully tip-tilted nose powdered chalk-white, like mine. My confidence had begun to ebb as I viewed our two partners: Richard Norton and Archie Campbell, both in uniform and wearing monocles, and both with an aura of social success about them, beyond the orbit of a débutante.

What use were these two going to be to me afterwards,

egotistically, I wondered, as we sat down to dinner? Already, I knew that Richard was in love with Jean and nearly all the older girls I knew loved Archie. Jean and Richard would dance all night together and Archie would have to distribute his favours among his ardent following, which would keep him busy. Would Lady Kinloch introduce me to some men? I hoped she would. Otherwise, I seemed doomed to sit beside her.

We reached the dance and I danced once with Archie. Thereafter, returning reluctantly to the chaperons' bench, I found that Lady Kinloch had migrated to the bridge-table. Richard and Jean had disappeared and I knew no one else. Plumping for better luck, I took up my stance in the doorway.

The wearing of gloves has given me confidence, ever since. I like to think they give me an air of sophistication, especially if they have four buttons on each hand. For a non-smoker these give occupation.

That evening, I varied the procedure. Sometimes, I took off my gloves, or buttoned them up, in the doorway; sometimes I repeated this process in the cloakroom. Each movement I made as slow as possible. The cloakroom attendants were kind and greeted me with feigned surprise, each time I returned to them. And once, one of them gave me a glass of water.

I tried not to count the number of dances I had missed but they were mounting up. They seemed to go slower after they had passed twelve. By this time the backs of my legs were aching and I was ravenously hungry. Another hour went by and the dances now numbered sixteen.

About two in the morning, an old gentleman came up the stairs. Driven to desperate measures, determinedly I confronted him. 'Excuse me, sir,' I said, with the courtesy Mamma had taught me to use towards elderly strangers. 'Would you ask me to dance?'

For a minute he looked piercingly at me, and then he smiled. 'Charmed, Madam,' he answered.

He remained my cavalier until Lady Kinloch appeared and

thanked me charmingly as he bade me 'good night'. Should I ever see him again, inwardly I vowed that I would accost him at the beginning rather than at the end of the evening.

By contrast, Dodo Donaldson's brother did not seem nearly so attractive. His hands were damp with sweat and beads of it ran down into his eyes. After a maze of complicated steps and twirls and pirouettes, I suggested that we should sit down and talk. But, by this time, I had become guileful. 'Tell me about yourself,' I said. 'Have you always been a soldier?'

Unlike his brother, Olly Donaldson appeared to be more artistic than sexy. Clearing his throat, he began: 'Before the war I used to draw but now I've forsaken the Pen for the Sword.'

I had brought it on myself, but his reminiscences ought to last for at least two dances. Any partner was better than no partner, so I composed myself to listen to his early struggles at the Slade School.

Now Papa was training another battalion in Ireland, a composite battalion of the Highland Light Infantry. The incompatible elements between Northern and Southern Ireland now were strained to bursting point. In the North allegiance to His Majesty's Government was rigorously upheld by the Lord Lieutenant (Lord Wimborne) and his staff. But, in the South, the Sinn Feiners were winning over more and more supporters to their declared objective of Irish independence. And Papa wrote that he was longing to leave Ireland before he and his men were roped in as policemen.

There was no longer any question of our joining him for a holiday in Connemara. Apart from the risk to casual travellers (had we got there), food and travel restrictions were now so tight that probably the authorities would have forbidden us to enter the country.

At home, some compulsory food rationing had now been introduced and the menus in the restaurants had been cut down to one or two courses. Both restaurants and theatres closed early and, as far as outward appearances showed anything, night descended swiftly on fitfully sleeping cities.

And yet, behind shuttered windows, hilarious parties took place nightly, with rather an hysterical emphasis on 'giving the boys a good time'. Night-clubs had long since sprung into being in all the big towns, where people took their own drink and took turns with the band in thumping away at the piano.

In London, despite the façade of chaperons, some of the girls I knew slipped away from the private parties they were supposed to be attending, to frequent some of these night-clubs, notably the Grafton Galleries. Frequently Loïs did, and one or two older girls. But, for some unknown reason, I and my cronies did not go; perhaps because we might have been distressed to find our own particular boy-friends entertaining glamorous chorus-girls. (Had this happened, sanctimoniously we would have found it hard to forgive them.) True, many of us envied Loïs, who Lady Alington had decreed should be chaperoned by Napier. (Unbeknownst to Lady Alington, in his turn, Napier turned over Loïs to the chaperonage of Miss Tallulah Bankhead and Miss Teddie Gerrard, but most of us realized that these Olympian heights were not for us.) Sometimes, I sighed wistfully when I thought of Edward but my two regular chaperons (Lady Harcourt and Lady Jessel) were charming to me and I had no cause for complaint. They had, on the other hand, for, having once got us to our parties, sometimes an air-raid would prevent us leaving, and both hostesses and chaperons were landed with having to make arrangements for the night.

Mamma found the solution to their difficulties, one day picking up a 'tame' taxi-man, who undertook to deliver and collect half a dozen débutantes to and from their destinations two or three nights weekly. At first we were elated by the change, but we soon found that we had to submit to Army discipline. If we gave Mr. Kemp a time to collect us he was there, air-raid or not, but woe betide us if we kept him waiting! He told us off like troopers, no matter who was there to hear.

And he saw off any of our escorts who sought to see us home. 'Now then, 'op it!' he would say. 'I'm 'ere to see the girls 'ome to their ma's, not to go with you.'

Despite the restrictions and anxieties, we were all enjoying ourselves, subject only to our ever-present worry that our escorts would in due course be called to active service.

Now I went round with a little 'clique' of girl-friends: Enid Dudley-Ward, Marjorie Jessel, Doris Harcourt, Lindy Benson, Marjorie Jenkins. And usually the same set of young men accompanied us: Allan Adair, Eric Stocks, Roger Wright, Jackie Phillips (when they were home on leave), Dick Curzon, Jim Fitzgerald, Stephen Burroughs. Mr. Kemp's vigilant eye was trained on us most evenings, but a concession to liberty was granted us at tea-time, when, as long as other girls were there, we were allowed to entertain young men in our own houses without a chaperon. In the daytime, we were still accompanied in the street by a maid or governess but, again at tea-time, two girls together were allowed to share a taxi.

When I went away to stay, Nannie accompanied me, un-wrapping and handing me over to my hostess and receiving me back, wrapped up again, as though I were a parcel.

Most of my friends were in Guards Regiments based in and around London, but sometimes I migrated outside the orbit of the Brigade of Guards, as when I stayed with Mrs. Jenkins for a Greenjacket Dance in Winchester. Mrs. Jenkins was an angel of kindness but she took her chaperoning duties seriously, and her distress was evident when I elected to spend that even-ing with a fascinating stranger (I think temporarily attached to the Rifle Brigade) whose slightly bloodshot, bold, black eyes proclaimed him an expert in feminine seduction. So worried did she become that she telephoned to Mamma next morning, warning her to expect trouble. Out walking with Mamma a day or two later, to my delight suddenly I saw the black-eyed Major advancing towards us down Grosvenor Street, accom-panied by a bloodhound. Hardly had I time to ejaculate his name before Mamma whisked me into No. 16 and shut the door in his face. So quickly did she act that, to this day, I do not know if the Major and his bloodhound had tracked me down deliberately.

One shared joy at this time was the news that Rupert Keppel had been released as prisoner of war, and was now interned in Holland. There, fortunately Papa's brother-in-law (Uncle Walter Townley) was British Minister at the Hague, so Rupert was able to go straight to the British Legation, there to be nursed back to health by Aunt Susan. At this time, regardless of her personal safety, Daisy spent much of her time on the high seas, going backwards and forwards between England and Holland, where she did invaluable work for the internees. Through her (as well as Aunt Susan) Uncle Arnold and Aunt Gertie got rather worrying reports about Rupert. He had very much changed, after forty months' imprisonment, she said and had lost most of his erstwhile gaiety. The re-introduction of Rupert into the family circle had an odd effect on me, rather as if, suddenly, an older photograph had been pulled more into the forefront, to take the place of a newer one.

Now, I had a new job, as pantry-maid to the Russian Hospital for Officers in South Audley Street. (This had been generously equipped and handed over by Monsieur Moura-vieff, erstwhile Chamberlain to the Czar, who had had to flee from Russia with his family at the time of the Revolution.) At seven o'clock each morning, Marjorie Jessel and I presented ourselves for duty, preparing breakfast-trays and washing-up and only rarely rising from the basement to the ground floor. All the pantry-maids called each other by their surnames over a rattle of cups and saucers, and not one of us had an inkling of the private life of the other.

Without really noticing it, the back-cloth of all our home lives had very much changed. In order to finance the war now the Government had a much bigger pull in purchasing power and on prices; there had been two big loans the year before and a big diversion to the State of the profits of commerce and industry. On the basis of economy now the Government were reorganizing the railways, and semi-nationalizing the mines. And the fusion of the five big Banks had already begun in 1917, which was to have a big effect on the post-war financial world. Although I took in very little of all this, I was fully aware of the renewed appeal for War Loan in February 1918, and of the Government's already heavy borrowing from America. Mamma and Winston and her other great friend, Reggie McKenna, frequently discussed the necessity for these decisions before me, which they emphatically agreed had become inevitable.

The actual war news seemed better. The submarine menace was less and new shipping was at last filling up former losses and, in France, nothing very spectacular seemed to be happening. Recently, there had been another 'call-up' at home (this time of men between 40 and 45) preceded by an ever tightening policy of 'combing-out' Civil Servants and munition workers from reserved occupations. And there was a growing feeling that very soon now huge American reinforcements would be with us. Then, terrifyingly, there was a sudden break-through of the German army, in April. The shock of it forced the Allies to make realistic decisions and, at long last, their joint troops were unified into one command, under General Foch. But only just in time.

In sheer contrast to the now pervading austerity, in August that year (just after another desperate attempt at a German break-through and amid a generally depressing atmosphere of strikes) I went to stay with Sir Hedworth Williamson, erstwhile hero of that nightmarish matinée long ago, when the lady behind him had pinned him to his seat with her hat-pin.

Walking into Appley Hall, Ryde, Isle of Wight, was like walking into a scene of classical revelry by Rubens. Both house and garden were crammed to overflowing with well-rounded statues; 'putti'; rococo chairs; tables; fountains; beds; musical instruments; plants; most of them smothered under cushions and drapery. The walls of each room were lined with curvaceous Watteau shepherdesses and Boucher nymphs. At intervals in the garden one came on stone images of Pan or Adonis, and figures of Cupid and Psyche. Over all this petrified pursuit of Love Hedworth presided, a genial Dionysus, living mainly on milk. Ostensibly, his life seemed to be dedicated to a worship of pagan fecundity, and yet he was a conscientious churchman, and a great upholder of the sanctity of marriage (by proxy). In actual fact, I think his life was genuinely dedicated to classical beauty of form, whether in human shape, or verse, or music, or well-rounded phrases. He disliked angularity and sparse outline and only tolerated it in Lady Elizabeth and his niece, Elizabeth, because they were his relations. He liked people to be sleek and well-fed, like cats, and whenever possible his food had a cream basis. This had become very difficult of achievement by the time I arrived at Appley and sometimes I suspect that he had to meet it synthetically, with soya bean and marshmallow.

Nowhere was his benevolent eccentricity more apparent than in the elaborate preparations he made to take his guests bathing. At the foot of his garden was a ruined tower and this he had fitted up for the ladies as a sort of moated grange, equipped with coffers of strangely assorted bathing dresses, and garlands of ivy leaves, and long tresses of bright yellow gun-cotton hair. With these, we were supposed to bedeck ourselves before pursuing him across the public highway into the sea. This might not have been too embarrassing if Hedworth himself had not looked so extraordinary, in a long black tunic down to his ankles and a toga of white Turkish towelling slung from his shoulder. Why no one ever arrested us as lunatics I shall never know. Probably the authorities held back because Hedworth was very well loved in Ryde, where his generosity and invariable kindness far outstripped his eccentricity.

Throughout the war years he ran a concert party to amuse wounded soldiers, roping in and producing the most unsuspected talent, and convulsing everyone by his own genius for burlesque. His nieces, Phyllis Herbert and Elizabeth Williamson, and I were all pressed into his service that August, and I had had only a few hours' rehearsal before I found myself playing 'Fair Cat' opposite Phyllis Herbert as 'Dark Cat', in 'The Rest Cure', for the first time in my life.

After a day or two of such masquerading, the extraordinary appeared quite usual and at night I sank to sleep in a rococo conch-shell as easily as though it had been a crib.

At eleven o'clock on the morning of November 11th, the maroons sounded and, this time, it meant an armistice, not an air-raid. For a second Violet and I looked at each other, then we both screamed: 'Moiselle!' and then: 'Barbelion!'

Having hugged Moiselle as a newly-discovered ally, we rushed out, hatless, to Bond Street to the French sweetshop, 'Barbelion', where we submitted the staff to the same enthusiastic treatment and dragged most of it with us towards Piccadilly.

Within the space of minutes, the street was packed tight with taxis and buses and, here and there, staff cars, all of them immediately overrun by streams of hysterically cheering people. Still firmly grasping Madame Barbelion by the arm, Violet and I boarded a taxi already crammed to capacity with girls and soldiers. They made way for us on the roof and we clung on perilously, still shouting: 'Vive la France!' Down Bond Street we crawled, neck to neck with the next-door taxi calling to strangers as though they were brothers, treating our progress like a Battle of Flowers. Arrived at Piccadilly, Violet and I got separated, she turning right with Madame Barbelion towards the Ritz, I continuing down St. James's Street with two sailors, an Army Chaplain, and a nurse. On the way down, I recognized Rex and Lindy coming up, and again I switched taxis, joining forces with them and Count Willie de Grün, a Belgian friend. We decided to go to the Carlton Hotel to celebrate, and eventually arrived there to find it milling with

EDWARD,
1917

ROLIE,
1918

SAN MORITZ, 1920

people in an atmosphere jointly reminiscent of a Hunt Ball and a wedding, all laughing and toasting each other, like long-lost relations. We joined in the toasts: 'To France!' 'A l'Angle-terre!' 'Les braves Belges!' The excitement rose to fever pitch as Rex picked up Willie and put him on a table, screaming: 'Voici le brave Belge, lui-même!' We could see tears in Willie's eyes behind his glasses, and everyone within reach toasted him and many women tried to pull him down to kiss him. Somehow we managed to find something to eat, and then we were off again, struggling towards Trafalgar Square, to Nelson's Column where we had a sudden urge to pay homage, in gratitude for our continued freedom of the seas. Throughout the day we formed part of the crowd, purposeless, happy, with no thought of the cares of tomorrow, or of the worries that Peace might bring.

In the evening we stood outside Buckingham Palace, cheer-ing our King and Queen with voices hoarse with hours of cheering, linking arms with the strangers around us, vowing eternal fealty to everyone we saw. Later, still in our tumbled day clothes, we went on to a party where the hostess threw open her doors to the people outside so that her invited and uninvited guests could mix merrily together. Every face shone with happiness and good fellowship and there did not seem to be a single flaw in the general felicity on that wonderful day.

But two sad contrasts were revealed later. Stephen Bur-roughs was killed by a stray bullet, just after the 'Cease fire' sounded; and, at Crichel, also on Armistice Day, Gerard Sturt died, in the arms of his valet.

PART FIVE

The Final Move

Chapter Fourteen

KALEIDOSCOPIC LENS

THE WAR was over and now most of us only saw what we wanted to see and turned a blind eye on further unpleasantness. At the General Election in December, Mr. Lloyd George had promised to preserve the bonds of comradeship between classes which had been welded in war, and we had all been relieved to hear him say this, and to know that he did not contemplate a return to party politics in the immediate future. A Coalition Government came in again and we all hoped that it would see to the demobilization of five million men, as soon as possible. This, and the need to find jobs for them, took up much more of our attention than the Sinn Fein declaration of a 'Republican Parliament' in Ireland; or the miners' strikes which broke out soon after. The war was still too near to us to let us forget the gratitude we owed to the men who had won it. When their demobilization appeared to be unjustifiably delayed, we supported their outcry, which became so persistent that, piecemeal, the Government had to do something about it.

At last, Papa had got away from Ireland and now he was A.D.C. on General Barnes's personal staff in France. Repeatedly, I wrote him to get himself demobilized soon so that he could come back to chaperon me to dances. He appeared to be in no great hurry to do so. Indeed, he was one of the few who seemed pleased still to be in the Army. 'What job can I find, when I do come back?' he asked. 'Nothing that a younger man wouldn't do much better. The work is most interesting out here, with Reggie Barnes, and I'll stick on as long as he wants me.'

I was puzzled and rather hurt by his attitude. Did he not want to become a family man again, now that the war was over?

Early in 1915, my godmother, Maggie Greville, had turned most of her house (Polesden Lacey, near Dorking) into a Convalescent Home to King Edward VII's Hospital for Officers. She had kept back the east side, and her own rooms fronting on the south side, for her private use.

In any generation, Maggie would have been outstanding. The daughter of a shrewd old Scottish brewer, from her earliest years she had taken an interest in his business, mastering the intricacies of its processes and management until eventually she won for herself a seat on the Board through her own business acumen. Always, she had loved power, in her youth sipping it, in small draughts, in her father's office in Edinburgh; later (with his money behind her), savouring it, in its social context, in the drawing-rooms of Europe. In 1891 she had married Papa's greatest friend, Ronnie Greville, eldest son of Lord Greville, a charming unambitious man whom she moulded affectionately into any shape she pleased. Papa always said that she was devoted to Ronnie and that, had they had children, she would have given up much of her social life to be with them. Unquestionably she was fond of them and, in my extreme youth, had wanted to adopt me. When Mamma had refused to let me go always she remained near enough at hand to be a delightfully indulgent godmother. But, when no child of her own materialized, she took up her pursuit of power again (preferably, beside a throne), firmly conducting Ronnie through the lobbies of politics until two years before his death, in 1908. Throughout most of Kingy's reign I can see her, small but forceful, making her way to the front of any company she was in. But Papa said that, after Ronnie died, she mourned him sincerely for a long time. Then Kingy himself died, but this interval of her mourning was shorter. Soon she was back near the throne of the new King and Queen, a person to be reckoned with and courted in any strata of society.

Maggie's main grace was that she was interested in people. A success snob it is true, she did not mind at what level she found it. Nowadays, I feel sure that she would have constantly reviewed the Personnel Department in her breweries. And throughout her life, she produced hitherto anonymous but intelligent men whom she had picked up, in some remote part of the globe, because she thought they administered their jobs efficiently. When she had done so, she expected them to let her run their lives and those who were clever enough pretended to let her do so.

The Convalescent Home at Polesden was run on luxurious lines and it is amusing to think that a young Australian officer, Tommy Fairfax-Ross, was first sent there as a penance for supposed insubordination to Sister Agnes Keyser, the formidable matron of King Edward VII's Hospital.

Tommy (T.) had joined the Rifle Brigade at the age of seventeen and had been twice wounded by the time he got to Polesden. His 'insubordination' had taken the form of an outspoken row with Sister Agnes and her doctors over what he considered the slow progress of his recovery.

He, and his brother-convalescent officers, lived on the west and south sides of the house, together with a resident staff of nurses and orderlies. On the private side Maggie entertained the notabilities of the moment, together with a regular nucleus of ambassadors, peers and politicians.

Maggie took all her responsibilities seriously and already she had discussed with Mamma the advisability of finding me a 'suitable' husband. Mischievously, Mamma told me this so that I was on the 'qui vive' to discover Maggie's current choice, whenever I went to Polesden.

The trouble was that she mixed up my possible suitors, as though in a bran-pie, regardless of age, and very often I failed

to discern them. The first time I went General Smuts was there
(but he had a wife) and Sir John Simonds (but he had another).
True, there had been rather an elderly peer (very interested in
golf), and Sir John Cowans, neither of whom was married.
But they had seemed very old and certainly neither of the
bachelors had seemed interested in me, as a bride. Sir John
had offered to give me a photograph-album but I did not
think that even Maggie could consider that a pledge of be-
trothal.

So I had wandered round the terrace to the west side, where
I had found T. hobbling along on crutches. 'Hallo!' he had
said. 'Are you out on parole?' 'Just about,' I had answered. I
had remained with him most of the afternoon and by contrast,
Maggie's guests had seemed very staid and heavy, when I
rejoined them, for tea.

As T. was intelligent (and still fairly anonymous), Maggie
took to him and became his lifelong friend, and soon she was
pulling wires to get him a good job, on discharge from the
Army. He got one (not through her) at the Peace Con-
ference and went back and forth to Versailles. And during that
time I, and my collection of friends, saw a lot of him.

Regardless of his own feelings on the subject, a few months
later, Marjorie Jessel and I divulged to each other that we were
both greatly attracted to T. and how were we to proceed
about him? As friends? Or rivals? At the time, we were walking
down Grosvenor Place and we decided to toss for him, on the
pavement. Producing a sixpence, I spun it and then put my
foot on it as it fell to the ground. 'Tails, I win; heads, I lose,'
I said, and won.

But, much as she liked T., I did not tell Maggie of this
action of mine. She would not have approved of it or, at least,
not for another thirty years or so, by which time T. should
have picked up a fortune.

The first big event of the London Season of 1919 was the
Victory Charity Ball, at the Albert Hall. At it, every Dominion

and Colony was represented by a leader and cortège of supporting maidens, all doing homage to the central figure of Britannia (I think represented by Mary, Lady Curzon). She, in her turn, was surrounded by chivalrous and heraldic figures; sailors; soldiers; airmen; figures of English history; Allies. Each Dominion represented their own major industry: Australia, in elaborate head-dresses and dresses trimmed with sheepskin; Canada, with a theme of wheat. The processions seemed unending, converging on Britannia, isolated on her dais above them, from doorways north, east, south and west. A dance floor had been laid down (subsequently to be danced on by three thousand dancers) and this was encircled by private boxes and tiers of seats. At the outset, Britannia dominated the centre of the scene, in an unenviable situation of complete solitude, shivering in a sheath of chiffon under her breastplate and in a howling draught.

I no longer remember the qualifications for selection required by each leader, but as far as I know the lady representing the granaries of Canada had no qualifications other than maturity and a bounteous heart. As a great friend of Mamma's she shall remain nameless, and no doubt the ties of her friendship inspired her kindly to include me in her cortège, as an ear of wheat.

About a dozen wheat-ears were to walk (or blow along) behind her and these she thoughtfully fed beforehand, at the Ritz. Other friends of hers made up her party and the transport of such a large number would have worried anyone other than her husband (a General of great tactical ability), to whom it seemed to present no problem whatsoever. In a jiffy he had allocated his guests to various cars and taxis, finally surprisingly allocating me to a seat beside him, in a brougham. 'Your dear Mother said you must be properly chaperoned,' he told me. 'So, who better to chaperon you than myself?'

Very much in awe of the General, I rattled off beside him, devoutly hoping that the nausea that used to affect me in childhood would not affect me in a brougham again. The

General was a big man and broad in proportion and, as we bowled past Bath House, in Piccadilly, he made a plunge at my throat.

The onslaught was so unexpected that I was knocked off balance, hitting my head a painful blow against the window-frame. Any early feelings of nausea evaporated in a surge of rising anger and all awe of the General vanished as I scratched his face.

'What a little tigress it is!' he exclaimed delightedly. 'Quite able to fend for itself really, without a chaperon!'

'I'll—I'll tell Papa about you!' furiously, I stammered. 'And I expect he'll horsewhip you!' To which the General replied, chuckling: 'In order of rank in the Army, that would be *most* unwise!'

With silent intensity I fought him all the way down Piccadilly to Hyde Park Corner, and through Hyde Park to Alexandra Gate. By the time we arrived at the Albert Hall I do not know which of us was the victor. One wheat-ear was down and the other stood up erect on my head like a prawn in rigor mortis; much of the powder had gone from my nose and there was a rent in the drapery on my shoulder through which showed a large black bruise. On the other hand, the General's face was criss-crossed with red scratches, and his swollen left thumb showed my teeth-marks in it clearly, where I had bitten it. As the brougham drove up to the entrance, he looked at me and burst out laughing. 'Never enjoyed a drive so much in my life!' he exclaimed. 'Now, run along, and tidy up, before I hand you over.'

When the cloakroom attendant had made me presentable again, thereafter I felt compelled conscientiously to carry out my duties as a wheat-ear to the General's wife. The procession appeared to go quite smoothly but, directly it came to an end, I found Mamma in her box and asked to go home.

'Don't you feel well, darling?' solicitously, she asked me, as we pursued our now peaceful way homewards, across the Park.

'I think my chaperon, the General, has cracked one of my ribs,' I answered, still resentfully. 'Otherwise, I suppose I feel all right.'

Just once, Mamma broke her rule, and presented me at one of Their Majesties' Summer Courts. And Papa accompanied us, in uniform. In a parure of diamonds which had belonged to Marie Antoinette and with a tiara of diamonds on her head, Mamma looked wonderful and, to me, she and Papa still eclipsed all the other parents in beauty. Doris, Marian Glyn, my cousin Anne Keppel (Uncle Derek's daughter) and I were all presented together, feeling very much like a parade of circus ponies, with the Prince of Wales's feathers on our heads.

My presentation dress came from Reville & Rossiter, in Hanover Square, and was made of pale pink tulle, with a brocade and silver train. The personality of Mr. Reville always intrigued me as, apart from being an expert dress designer, he was also an expert on Chinese art. As one came into the shop, a large part of the left side of it was divided off by curtains, sumptuously embroidered with Chinese dragons, behind which one had an occasional tantalizing glimpse of a large gilt Buddha and walls draped in black. Wild rumour had it that, behind the Buddha, Mr. Reville had an opium den and Mamma told me never to accept an invitation from him to go behind the curtains. Had I done so, probably I would have found the poor little man having a comforting cup of tea with his staff. As it was, every time I fitted my dress, like Fatima, I was devoured by curiosity as to what the embroidered dragons hid.

To the envy of my girl-friends, Mr. Reville prevailed on Mamma to let me have hardly any sleeves. Up till then, we all had draped bits of net, or chiffon, or the stuff the dress was made of, concealing the outlines of our shoulders. The rest of the dress was plain and, as far as possible, flat-chested, with my bosom kept within Spartan bounds underneath it by a broad band of satin ribbon. This restriction was essential as, at that time, we all tried to obliterate our feminine curves. In antithesis to the fashion, about twelve years earlier, when every woman had sought to accentuate them.

Buckingham Palace itself exceeded all my expectations of magnificence. Besides the glitter of a stage-set, it had substance and reality. It seemed remarkable to me that we were all playing actual parts, by tradition, in this Ceremony of Presentation. No queues for theatre-tickets; no Box Office; just the time-honoured right to apply for free admittance to meet our King and Queen. Old-fashioned and dry though it had seemed, probably 'Little Arthur's History of England' had subconsciously prepared my mind for this moment. And certainly Mr. Ford's colourful lectures had helped it. But it was with 'A Kiss for Cinderella' uppermost in my thoughts that, nervously, I curtsied. And the thing that still impressed me most about Their Majesties was their accessibility.

The next chaperon Mamma appointed was Lady Lowther.

This lady was American-born, and the widow of a British Ambassador. She invited me to attend my first Ascot (in 1919) with her house-party, near Maidenhead.

Again, Mamma took infinite trouble over my clothes, buying me a new dress, hat, shoes and gloves, for each of the four days' racing. Cup Day I was to be magnificent (if rather overladen) in a cream-coloured lace dress, bronze shoes and bag, long cream-coloured suede gloves and, topping it all, a large dark brown straw hat trimmed with sweeping Bird of Paradise feathers.

Now, Violet and I shared a Studebaker car (more mine than hers as she refused to drive it). Some time before, Reggie McKenna's nephew, Stephen, had written a novel called 'Sonia', so my car was called 'Stephen', and in 'Stephen' I set out for Ascot, accompanied by Mamma's chauffeur, Hyde, and Nannie (quite a cortège for a girl of 19!).

By now, most of Mamma's women friends seemed to have taken a vow to find me a 'suitable' husband. Their interpretation of the term seemed to cover a widening field, Lady Lowther's selection falling on the Grand Duke Dmitri Pavlovitch, of Russia.

Together with his brother-in-law, Prince Yussupoff, in 1916, this glamorous young man had acquired worldwide notoriety through his share in the murder of Rasputin. With the deliberate intention of ending the evil power of this sinister priest, on a cold December night Prince Yussupoff had invited Rasputin to supper at his palace in St. Petersburg where he had found the Grand Duke Dmitri, and half a dozen others, assembled to meet him. First, they had tried to poison him with cyanide mixed in his drink, to no effect; then, so rumour had said, a member of the party had shot him. Later, they had pushed his body through the ice, into the River Neva.

The Grand Duke was hardly a 'suitable' choice for an English girl of nineteen but, as can be imagined, I was thrilled at the prospect of meeting him. He arrived late on the Wednesday evening, just before dinner, and asked for drinks to be sent up to his room while he dressed. In due course, the rest of the party assembled downstairs and at first, no comment was made on His Imperial Highness's unpunctuality. Then, after an hour's wait, the hostess herself said that dinner would be spoilt, and felt that she must go up to find out what was happening.

At intervals during our wait, strange sounds had reached us from the Grand Duke's room above. Apparently, it was his valet's practice always to dress him and, at first, loud laughter and a clinking of glasses had been heard; then, scuffling, a few shouts, and then silence. As Lady Lowther mounted the stairs, bangings on the door began, accompanied by louder and increasingly angry shouts. After some time, she managed to extract the information that the Grand Duke had locked his door on the inside and had broken the key in the process.

By this time, we were all assembled outside his room and alarming thoughts were running through my mind. Had the Grand Duke poisoned his valet's drink with cyanide and was the wretched man now writhing in agony on the floor? Or had he shot him with a muffled bullet, and, even now, was trying to dispose of the body through the window?

With mounting hunger, we listened to the kicks and flow of Slav invective. Then some bright spark said: 'Send for a carpenter, and saw a hole through the door!'

Lady Lowther had taken the house for Ascot Week and was not keen to pay heavy damages. When the carpenter arrived, she instructed him to cut out one small panel only, at the bottom.

Through this, finally crawled the Heir of all the Russias looking like a bear, on all fours, followed by his valet. Hawk-eyed, I examined the valet, who did not look too bad. But he gave me a shock again, next morning, when I saw him lying on the door-mat outside his master's room, possibly protecting him from renewed onslaughts from the carpenter.

That evening was disrupted but, for me, the next day was superb. Escorted through the paddock at Ascot by one of the celebrities of Europe (now immaculately clad in lavender-grey frock coat and white top hat), I preened my Bird of Paradise feathers beside him. When any of my friends came up, with studied unconcern, I introduced him. He was not all that easy to talk to, and sometimes I was glad to change his company for one of my cosier boy-friends. (These too, looked very smart, in uniform.) But, undoubtedly, his presence at my side most of the day was the envy of my girl-friends.

No doubt with Lady Lowther's full approval, later the Grand Duke took me on the river. But my native caution made me refuse his invitation to dine with him at Skindles. Spiced drinks and cyanide. . . . One never knew. And I could not be sure that, after dark, he would not mistake the Thames for the Neva.

Two family weddings marked the first six months of 1919. On January 29th, Rupert's to Vi de Trafford; and, on June 16th, Violet's, to Denys Trefusis.

Rupert's marriage to Vi was the fulfilment of **a long**

romance. He had loved her before he went to the war, in 1914, and her image had sustained him throughout his forty months of imprisonment. On his return from Holland, in November 1918, from all accounts Vi must have found him very much altered. And obviously she too had changed, though Rupert professed not to notice it. I can remember very little of the circumstances of their wedding except packed pews either side of the aisle; and (as Vi was a Catholic and Rupert Church of England) that they were married without any singing.

I was very much surprised by Violet's choice of Denys, as a husband. Since Julian, she had favoured predominantly literary and artistic types, to whom war had come as an incongruous occupation. But, although not markedly of a military disposition, practically from the first moment I saw him, Denys impressed me as a soldier. He had a Crusader's flare to his nostrils and a cold, bright eye which I felt would unhurriedly size up an enemy. And the same cold, bright eye had travelled over my face, as though studying a map of reconnaissance. An officer in 'The Blues' at the outset of war, Denys had gone out to France and had fought through the retreat from Mons and the first battle of Ypres until he had been gassed near Ypres in 1915. This had left him with an almost imperceptible breathlessness which made any remark he made sound impatient.

At first, I did not like him much, as he was not forthcoming. No avowals of deep love for Violet; no protestations of fidelity. I think that Mamma and Papa and I had all three expected him to make some declarations of this kind or, at least, to be demonstrative to Violet, in front of us. When he neither said nor did anything that could not have been said or done in the open street, we all felt rather frustrated. Yet, reputedly, a lot of women had been in love with Denys and he was very popular with men, largely because he kept his own counsel. And Violet herself behaved differently, when she was with him: dressing carefully, making much bigger efforts to please. Obviously, he improved on acquaintance so I decided to wait, and to reserve my opinion of him until I knew him better.

More than anything, Violet's wedding reconciled Papa to demobilization. He got out his invitation-book again, bringing its columns up-to-date, adding many new names of soldier friends made in the war and military pips to a lot of the 'Old Men' (my pouncing General among them). And he put a sad red line through many of the 'Young Men' (including dear Edward). He thought out every detail of transport; allocation to the pews, in church; music; champagne, at the reception. He only left the bridesmaids' dresses and the flowers, for Mamma to do; and the cake and buffet refreshments, all made by Perriat. Most of all he concentrated on the music in the church. He commissioned a friend of his, an organist of great talent, to play Purcell's 'Trumpet Voluntary' before the arrival of the bride and, during the signing of the register, Dame Nellie Melba herself sang Gounod's 'Ave Maria', as an anthem. When Violet and Denys came down the aisle, the same organist played the Wedding March from 'Lohengrin'. It seemed to me that the exquisite music was Papa's own special send-off to Violet.

January 29th and June 16th, 1919: two wedding-congregations, one mute, one full-throated. But both praying, with the same degree of sincerity, for the happiness of the bride and bridegroom.

Chapter Fifteen

FAMILY INTRODUCTIONS

THE FIRST time I saw Rolie he filled me with alarm as he was wringing the nose of a very pretty girl, at a party. The nose took it well and the owner of the nose took it better still but I realized that I would have fiercely resisted such an onslaught.

At that time our partners were continually changing, through drafting overseas, but the old 'Square' formation of the Brigade of Foot Guards in battle still seemed to be preserved in the ballroom and, when one member of it went overseas, automatically another seemed to move forward to replace him. Now, only the wounded or very young were left as replacements, of whom Rolie Cubitt, Jock Gilmour, Norman Gwatkin and Brecky (Brecknock) had all been due for drafting overseas just as the Armistice was signed.

Rolie himself had a background of major family tragedy as three of his elder brothers had been killed, by the time I met him. The fourth son out of a family of six boys, suddenly he had discovered himself the eldest of the remaining three with eldest son responsibilities he had never dreamt of assuming. In appearance he strongly resembled Jackie Phillipps, in their slim, dark blue tunics, at night, and their smart khaki, and in the day-time, at first I was inclined to look on them both as interchangeable.

Rolie's greatest charm was his gaiety. With his bright eyes and inexhaustible capacity for enjoyment, he looked like an alert fox terrier, eager for exercise. He did not mind where he got it (in the ballroom; out of doors) as long as his light feet could tune in to the steps of his friends. I had an idea that he preferred them to tread a known measure and (with a sudden strong list towards my Dryad-like aunts and their fears of the unexpected) I was glad of this. In him once again I recognized the qualities I liked best with, behind him, the country background I preferred. I was told that his parents lived in a large house in Surrey, looking towards Leith Hill and, in my imagination, I saw it as a mixture of Melbury and Quidenham, with smooth lawns running down to a lake perhaps, on which swans were majestically sailing. Inside the house I visualized mellow family portraits (possibly even with some kindred portraits by Sir Joshua) and the furniture almost inevitably would be a handing-down through the reigns of Queen Anne and the Georges to the last solid bits of Regency furniture in the bedrooms. I did not spend much time in anticipating the looks of Rolie's parents except that, obviously, they would be white-haired, poor things, because of their triple tragedy. What I saw with greater clarity was plenty of retrievers and an odd cocker spaniel or two, in the foreground and, away in the background, some large, well-fed horses in the stable. My ears took up the theme and, in the morning, I could hear the sound of the gardener's rake raking over the gravel in the drive and, later, rooks cawing in the tree tops as the sun went down. And, last thing before sleeping, I could hear an owl mysteriously hissing and hooting.

I began to invest Rolie himself with practically every romantic quality: Adonis's beauty; the chivalry of Sir Lancelot; the fidelity of Leander; the heroism of King Arthur. Being an essentially simple person, had he realized this he would have been extremely embarrassed by it and would have quickly divested himself of the trappings with which my fertile imagination clothed him. But I do not think that such a possibility even occurred to him. In his happy way he took people as he found them and expected them to do the same about him. So he did nothing to stop me and gradually the mental image

I formed of him became so idealized that no human being on earth could have lived up to it.

'Doey darling, why are you dressed up like that?' Sadie Greenwood asked me, when she met me one Saturday morning in Bond Street. And blushingly I replied: 'I'm going to stay with Rolie's parents for the week-end, at Denbies.'

Although the fashions were tending more and more towards a merging of the hem of our skirts with our waistlines, on that particular day I was dressed rather unusually. My skirt was several inches longer than the fashions decreed (Nannie had let it down specially); my hands were encased in white cotton gloves; and, with a big effort of renunciation, my nose was practically free of powder. Rather lugubriously, I peered at Sadie from under the brim of my large Leghorn hat. 'Marjorie Jessel says that Lady Ashcombe doesn't like "fashionable" girls, but that she does like them to wear gloves. Otherwise, she just likes them to look natural.'

Always kindness itself, Sadie laughed and said: 'She'll love you for what you are, Doey, not for what you wear.' But I was determined to take no chances.

Unofficially, Rolie and I had been engaged for nearly a year but still his parents were firm in their belief that we were 'too young to know our own minds.' And, surprisingly, Mamma agreed with them. When I had told her that Rolie and I were in love with each other and that he had asked me to marry him, to my distress, she had looked worried. 'It isn't that I don't like Rolie,' she had said, 'I think he's very nice. But if you marry him, you'll marry into a world you've never known, and I'm not at all sure that you'll like it.'

Giving him the responsibility of an elder son at the conclusion of war, Rolie's father had handed him over an old-fashioned limousine Panhard, very high off the ground, into which Marjorie Jessel, Jock Gilmour and I piled for our drive down to Denbies. Jock sat beside Rolie on the box while he drove us.

Marjorie knew Denbies already and beguiled the journey with a rather disjointed description of it. 'The drive is miles long and the house sits on top of the hill like a sanatorium. . . . Lord Ashcombe has family prayers every morning which of course I can't attend as I'm a Jewess. . . . The girls all have to wear gloves in the house all day. . . . No one is allowed to smoke in the drawing-room, or to play cards on Sundays. . . .

As the car turned into the drive, a slight chill struck me as the steep drive before us wound away upwards, like the hill Difficulty in *Pilgrim's Progress*. The ground began to fall away steeply to one side of us, gradually revealing a magnificent panoramic view with Dorking in the foreground. 'Goodness, what a view!' I said, but the chill persisted, associating itself with my sense of isolation, long ago, when I had looked at the seemingly endless vista of tea plantations from Dambatene.

'There's the sanatorium!' Marjorie said cheerfully, as the huge square house came into sight. 'It's built with a basement, like the Belgrave Square houses Tom Cubitt (the first Cubitt builder) designed.' On either side of the front door a red fungus stained the grey walls. 'Like bloodstains!' Marjorie commented, as we went indoors.

Across the hall, opposite the front door, was a stained glass window with an heraldic motif and, apparently, it did not open, as the air smelt slightly of mildew and damp waders. Along the base of the wall, curving round it at least twice, was a narrow glass case containing an enormously long, thick, knotted bone. 'The dorsal fin of a brontosaurus,' helpfully, Marjorie explained.

The old butler ahead of us threw open a door and announced us, and by this time I was so nervous that my hand trembled as I shook hands with my hostess.

As we sat down to tea I took a furtive glance at the room which was dominated by three life-size, full length portraits of Rolie's dead brothers. They looked kind but serious, like an impartial Selection Committee, and not at all like the laughing photographs of them that Rolie had showed me. Nearly all the furniture in the room seemed to be late Victorian and was upholstered in railway-carriage plush. (As I took my seat with my back to the window, irrepressibly, Marjorie whispered: 'Hope you won't feel sick with your back to the engine!') There was a potted palm behind a sofa in one corner of the room, and several small glass vases of flowers smothered in maidenhair fern, mostly carnations. A large Victorian plate-glass looking-glass surmounted the chimney piece in which I saw the whole party sombrely reflected.

Rolie's mother and father had the white hair I had anticipated; she wore hers pinned up on the top of her head and beneath it her enormous brown eyes wore a beguilingly child-like expression. He was going bald but in the shape of his small, pointed face and his nose I could see how much the fox terrier puppy resembled its father. Throughout tea, Lady Ashcombe referred to me in the third person singular. 'Will the young lady have sugar in her tea? Will the young lady have a scone and some home-made strawberry jam?' Half dead with fright, I had a feeling that, by these indirect references, she was inferring that I had been deprived of my passport.

A lovely summer evening drew us out of doors where, although there was no lake to fit in with a Melbury-cum-Quidenham setting, a beautiful beech wood provided a romantic background to a long lawn leading away to a church in the distance. We played tennis on a very good grass court and then gorged ourselves with strawberries, in the kitchen garden. By this time I had regained my self-confidence which I felt I could easily keep, if only I could remain out of doors. But the dressing-gong boomed out across the lawn and, panic-stricken, I raced Marjorie back into the house, fearful of creating a bad impression through unpunctuality.

Just before dinner, a housemaid brought me a pair of elbow-length, white kid gloves. 'His Lordship's compliments, miss, and will you please wear them.' My progress downstairs coincided with the other female members of the party, all similarly buttoning on new white kid gloves. Thus arrayed, we were all formally armed-in to dinner.

An enormous Landseer painting of a horse, a mule, a donkey and a St. Bernard covered the wall at the far end of the dining-room, where, again, the dining-room table and chairs were admirably designed to resist the strain of long board meetings of the Southern Railway.

It soon became clear to me that Lord and Lady Ashcombe liked the company of young people, and both of them seemed to sit back to enjoy Marjorie's sallies. After dinner we crowded round a jigsaw puzzle in the drawing-room, while Lord and Lady Ashcombe played patience at a small table in the corner. During the evening I hardly dared to look in Rolie's direction, and at ten o'clock precisely, Lady Ashcombe whisked Marjorie and me off to bed.

As the next day was Sunday, prayers did not take place, but every member of the party was expected to attend church, at eleven. Wearing a surplice, Lord Ashcombe sat in the Choir, and most of his male employees seemed to sit with him. He read the Lessons in a meek, submissive voice very much at variance with Uncle Arnold's voice when reading them, which boomed out as though it were rallying troops in battle. Yet, though Lord Ashcombe met it with bent head and Uncle Arnold with braced chest, there seemed nothing to choose between them in the way in which they endured tribulation.

When we came out of church we were greeted by vociferous barking from the various dogs awaiting us at the gate, and then proceeded, with the pack at our heels, to a detailed tour of the stables. Because of war restrictions, there were only two or three horses to inspect but we were given so much information about these that I felt I was attending a vivisection. We continued our walk on to a broad grass terrace which Rolie said had been copied from Polesden. But when I sought to build up this link with Polesden (which was only two miles away), Lady Ashcombe refuted the suggestion.

At luncheon another link bound Lord Ashcombe to Uncle

Arnold—his skill at carving. (Afterwards, when Rolie told me that his father was a chronic dyspeptic, I was not surprised, as, for years, the meat course must have been stone cold when it reached him.) The menus were written in English on white china stands and followed a daily formula. On Sundays, for luncheon, there was roast beef, a cream pudding, and Cheddar cheese, and for dinner, roast chicken, macédoine of fruit and trifle.

That Sunday afternoon, we played tennis again and came in for a large tea, and did not accompany Rolie's father and mother when they went back to church, in the evening. After dinner, we played 'Clumps' in the drawing-room.

Throughout the week-end I did not dare to think of the impression I was making on Rolie's parents and they gave no sign of any reaction to me. But I derived slight comfort from an unexpected incident on Monday morning. Still terribly nervous, somehow or other my restless hands got hold of a piece of knotted string which, unconsciously, I began to un- ravel. As she watched me, with sudden warmth in her voice, Lady Ashcombe commented: 'I like young ladies who undo string!' Dared I hope by that remark that she had decided to return me my passport?

Now, Mrs. Arthur James took a hand at trying to marry me off. Flanked by Nannie, I was sent off on a long, cold journey by train, to Coton House, near Rugby. Here, Mrs. James maintained (as she thought) despotic thrall over largely the same set of servants that I had known in Grafton Street. Went, the butler, was still there and Miss Barrow still ruled the housemaids. But, though they might give an impression of silent subjection to Mrs. James's ringing commands, in reality they continued quite imperturbably on their way, carrying out their duties with undeviated efficiency.

Since those dark, far-off days in 1910, I had developed a respectful affection for Mrs. James who had a stingingly salutary effect on me, like mustard in a bath of water. In some respects, she resembled Maggie Greville (a fact which would have annoyed them both): she had the same courage, the same mundane sense, I should say about the same income and, beneath the same outwardly hard surface, she had the same kind heart. In her case, her liking for power was domestically confined wherein she sought to rule her relations, her friends, her servants, those responsible for running her large stud of race-horses, and a mass of charitable institutions. And in another respect she differed very considerably from Maggie, and that was in her passion for small economies. Despite her wealth, in London she went by bus whenever she could and, in the country, on foot, in order to save petrol. At Coton, only her female guests were allowed fires in their bedrooms and her male guests had to endure their freezing rooms as best they could. At meals, she kept a sharp look-out for greed in her guests, and Went had strict instructions not to offer a second helping. Rather than employ a daily woman to come in to do the work, during some of her large week-end parties, sometimes she was seen coming out from the visiting valets' rooms over the stables, where she had nipped in to air their beds, after breakfast.

That November (1919) one of the easily discernible objects of her shooting-party was to bring off an engagement between Brecky (as Lord Camden's heir) and myself. To this end, we were put beside one another at meals and flung together between times. To and from church on Sunday morning she hurried on ahead of us, refusing to let us keep abreast, and only stopping once, on our outward way, unexpectedly to change shoes to alternate feet, because she said they hurt her less by so doing. In church (where Mrs. James played the organ and gave the congregation a deafening lead in the hymns) Brecky and I were made to sit in the same pew and made to share the same prayer-book.

Hail and sleet heralded in a glacially cold afternoon, which I hoped would dissuade Mrs. James from any attempt to amuse her guests out of doors. But mere weather could not dissuade her. Meaningly, she looked at Brecky and me and said: 'You two had better go for a bicycle ride, towards Rugby.' When we replied, with relief, that we had left our bicycles behind, triumphantly she announced that she had borrowed a housemaid's bicycle for me and a footman's bicycle for Brecky. Expostulation was useless so, with no hope of reprieve, dolefully, we departed on our way with Mrs. James's parting injunction ringing in our ears: 'You had better not come back till tea-time.'

About four miles away, Brecky's tyre burst and, of course, neither bicycle had a pump to inflate it. So there was nothing to do but to trudge back to Coton, pushing our bikes beside us. In spite of the numbing icy wind in our faces, which precluded much speech, now and then we giggled.

The joke was that Brecky had been engaged to Marjorie Jenkins for as long as I had been engaged to Rolie.

Chapter Sixteen

HOTEL ACCOMMODATION

IN THE same way that travellers on a pleasure cruise are flung together in a sudden spurious intimacy, so I, within twenty-four hours of Papa's and Mamma's and my arrival at the Palace Hotel, St. Moritz, found myself an integral part of its community life. I wore the same gaudily coloured sweater and tasselled cap and the same cumbersome ski-ing boots, and already I was a member of two bobsleigh teams, one with a crew of four men and myself, and the other with a crew of two men with myself as steerer. Twenty-four hours before these men had been unknown to me, yet now, here we were, threaded together on the same coloured strands of wool, preparing (on a dispassionate basis of height and avoirdupois) to risk our lives together.

After deciding to give me three weeks' holiday abroad, Mamma and Papa acted with their usual unselfish thoroughness. The evening of our arrival at the Palace Hotel, having fallen in with some old friends (the Duke of Alba and his brother-in-law and sister, the Duke and Duchess of Santona) they had put up a brief defence against Jack Santona's suggestion that I should take up bobsleighing during my stay there. Probably every phase of our first calamitous trip down the mountain side passed through Mamma's mind as she pointed out to him that I had absolutely no experience of bob-sleighing and had never before steered a boblet. But, when Jack airily waved such considerations aside neither she nor

Papa allowed their own misgivings to prejudice my pleasure. Once they had elicited from me that I was not frightened of the prospect (the dangers of which I had largely forgotten) they made no further difficulties, and, having taken the initial risk of taking me to St. Moritz for winter sports, they seemed fatalistically content to abide by it.

As steerer, the larger bobsleigh, 'Mixed Pickles', had a Swiss expert called Ammann, and the rest of the crew was made up of myself, an English army captain, Sir Edward Neylor-Leyland, and a Dutchman called Mr. Snooke. The two courageous men who gaily jeopardized their lives behind my inexpert hands in 'Chiffoneta' were Jack Santona and Prince Paul of Greece, whose height and weight were of great value as 'brake' to our boblet.

The Cresta bob-run was a very different affair to the village run Captain Dawson had attempted to negotiate nine years earlier. It had built-up sides, two curves of which (Sunny Corner and Horseshoe Corner) were sloped up to an approximate height of ten feet. Each night the run was sluiced with water which had frozen into solid ice by the morning. Down its serpentine length the distance of it was about two miles, on which a well-driven bobsleigh could achieve a speed of seventy miles an hour. (A good boblet speed reached about sixty). The 'Bobsleigh Derby' was the big event in the bobsleighing calendar and that year a Cup for boblets to compete for also had been presented by Prince and Princess Vlora of Rumania.

From the outset, there was no doubt in any of our minds that we intended to compete with both bobs, and Papa and Mamma accepted this cheerfully. Twice a day, they repaired to the spectators' seats at Sunny Corner, there to watch their daughter hurtling by, Mamma (as she told me afterwards) in audible prayer and Papa fiercely twirling his moustache to hide his emotion. The curve into Sunny Corner was too risky to be able to take my eye off the run but, somewhere in the crowd above it, I sensed their encouraging presence.

Both the 'Bobsleigh Derby' and the race for the Vlora Cup were two-day events and a lot of preliminary practice had to be put in. Mr. Ammann coached his team with purposeful brevity, much in the same way that yachtsmen train their sailing crews. Lying back prone behind him, he instructed us to keep our arms in to our sides and to lean into the curves as we came to them. The onus of speed devolved on to the brakesman who had to push us off and then jump on to the sleigh when in motion. Seven bobsleighs competed in the 'Derby' that year of which the most fancied were 'Excelsior', 'Yellow Peril' and 'Mixed Pickles'. I am ashamed to say that I no longer remember the names of the boblets competing for the Vlora Cup, although a fellow-steerswoman, Phyllis Lindsell, stands out in my mind very clearly. The 'bob' world was quite distinct from the 'ski' world and we kept very much together. Count Zoppola, steersman of 'Yellow Peril', took the lead (as confidently as he did in the ballroom).

At no time in my life have I achieved such crystal-clear clarity of mind as I did steering 'Chiffoneta'. Admittedly a case of needs must, from the instant the boblet started to move down the run my powers of concentration had to be tuned in to the slightest inference: a soft bit of snow on the track; a slightly different curve into 'Sunny'; the difficult and almost simultaneous alternation of balance out of 'Sunny' into the straight and in and out of 'Horseshoe' and then the final burst of speed down the hill. On a general basis one aimed to come fairly high into 'Sunny' and to keep low round 'Horseshoe Corner', but the momentum one had reached by that time made it difficult not to hit 'Horseshoe' too high, which meant that one was apt to run up the wall of ice above it. Once past 'Horseshoe', invariably, I breathed a sigh of relief knowing that, except for a bit of unusually bad luck, the worst was over.

Before both the 'Derby' and the race for the Vlora Cup, sweepstakes were held and high bids were made for the favourites. In the 'Derby', as I remember, 'Excelsior' was favourite, and in the Vlora Cup, to the excitement of the crew, 'Chiffoneta' was the most heavily backed. Both bobsleigh and boblet races were to follow the usual formula of one lap down the run on two consecutive days, leading off with the 'Derby'.

On the first lap of the 'Derby', 'Excelsior' led (with a time of one minute and forty seconds) over 'Yellow Peril'. A bob called 'Spatz' was third and 'Mixed Pickles' came in fifth, with a time of one minute, forty-three seconds. On the second day, 'Yellow Peril' drew level with 'Excelsior' and, in the final count, beat 'Excelsior' by one-fifth of a second. Much to the despondency of its crew, 'Mixed Pickles' finished fourth with an aggregate time of three minutes, twenty-six seconds.

The contest for the Vlora Cup started, and on the first day all was well. Both 'Chiffoneta' and Phyllis Lindsell's boblet finished ahead of the other contestants. 'Chiffoneta' had a slight lead over Phyllis's boblet with a time of two minutes ten seconds, but both were pretty evenly matched. On the second day, 'Chiffoneta' bettered her time by six seconds. Phyllis's boblet had drawn last place and, with our hearts in our mouths, my crew and I went down to see her come in at the finish.

Two miles away, over the vibrant air we heard the clang of the starter's bell, and Jack clocked in his stopwatch. With intense concentration, he, Prince Paul and I watched the second hand race round, followed by the fateful minute hand. One minute: two minutes; two minutes, five seconds; (we held our breath); ten seconds; twenty seconds; forty; sixty. Jubilantly, we turned to each other. Without doubt, we had won. Then Jack turned to look up the run again. Still clocking the time, he said: 'Four minutes; five minutes. She must have had an accident.'

Limbering our boblet on to the trailer at the back, we got into our horse-drawn sleigh and started back up the hill. And we did not have to go far before the news reached us. Phyllis's boblet had hit 'Horseshoe' too high and the whole thing had come over backwards. Under it, Phyllis's leg had been terribly crushed and, in an emergency operation later, she had to have it amputated.

I still have the Vlora Cup in my possession (the only cup I have ever won), and still I marvel that Providence should have guided me, rather than Phyllis, safely round Horseshoe Corner. At the time, the sports world at St. Moritz was horrified by the accident and, still held together by its community spirit, it showered Phyllis with gifts of flowers and fruit and queued up to visit her. While the holidays lasted she was the pet of the place. Then they came to an end and she was left behind, valiantly facing the future.

Two days before we were due to leave St. Moritz (on the next stage of our journey to Nice), Denys wired that Violet had a threatening of appendicitis. The telegram sounded urgent and Papa and Mamma decided to return to England at once, leaving me in Williams's care for twenty-four hours, and to be chaperoned by the Duchess of Santona. Already Jimmie d'Albe and his family had decided to travel with us to the South of France where, if Violet had sufficiently recovered by then, Mamma undertook to rejoin me. 'You'll be quite all right with Williams, darling,' she said, when I begged her to let me return to England too. 'No one ever dares to get in her way. She crosses the Alps like Hannibal.'

In our household, Williams had established a reign of terror ever since she had succeeded beloved Louise Draper five years earlier. In appearance, she looked like Queen Elizabeth (with more than a casual resemblance to Bloody Mary) and her character was much more in tune with the Middle Ages than with the twentieth century. She would have been astute in the Court intrigue of that time and relentless in almost any form of persecution. Then, as now, she would have had the doughty qualities required of that age, and she would not have depended on anyone but herself for advancement. And her desire to educate herself would have been as assiduous then as it was now.

She would have studied Erasmus and (with a determination to outmanœuvre the house-steward) almost certainly Euclid. Knowledge would have been her passport to betterment and woe betide anyone who disputed it.

On arrival in the South of France, Jimmie and his family were to visit his aunt, the Empress Eugénie, at Mentone, and Williams and I were to part from them there and go on to Nice, to Lady Nunburnholme's villa.

To the best of my ability, I kept out of Williams's way during the twenty-four hours that I was in her charge, realizing that even the most transitory status of 'young lady's maid' would be anathema to her. During that time, I gave Jimmie and Jack and Sol a pretty accurate picture of her. 'I see that I shall have to win Miss Williams's confidence,' Jimmie said in his faultless English. 'Otherwise she may refuse to travel with us.'

But to travel with a Grandee of Spain was just what Williams liked and especially one who (as Duke of Berwick as well as Alba) was directly descended from her own English King Charles II. As was to be expected, she knew much more about his lineage than I did. And the fact that he was going to stay with the Empress Eugénie also gave her considerable pleasure. 'To think of the money the Empress spent on her clothes!' she exclaimed to me. 'She used to get them from Worth, like Mrs. Keppel.'

Through shameless flattery to Williams, Jimmie ensured us all a very pleasant journey through Switzerland and, lulled into a false sense of security, we approached the Italian frontier. Just before we reached it he asked Williams to let him have her passport and mine. 'We shall get through the formalities quicker if I deal with all the passports,' he said. Unique in her travelling career, Williams ceded them without a murmur.

Casually, Jimmie turned over the pages, complimenting Williams on her photograph, laughing at mine. Then he went back and again carefully studied Williams's passport. 'Miss Williams,' he said, 'You have not had your passport visa'd for Italy!'

I was thankful that no one less than a Grandee of Spain had to acquaint Williams with this fact. A mere member of the English House of Lords would not have stood a chance against her vituperation. As it was, she grew scarlet, then gulped, then finally spoke. 'It's not possible, Your Grace!' she expostulated.

But Jimmie proved his point and, by now, the train was drawing to a standstill. 'You had better leave it to me to bluff you through,' he told Williams. 'Otherwise you won't be allowed across the frontier.'

With a sense of impending doom, Williams and I tagged along behind the others, she now as subdued as though she were about to be served with an Italian form of a 'lettre de cachet'. The frontier official appeared to be a voluble fellow and Jimmie engaged him in Italian, as fluently as he spoke English. By this time the man was looking through the passports and, suddenly, Jimmie seemed to burst into verse. Entranced the official paused, then, as Jimmie appeared to hesitate for a word, eagerly, he supplied it. He quoted something back to Jimmie and, between them, they seemed to go through quite a long stanza. At the end of it, the official realized he was pressed for time and shoved the remaining passports back into Jimmie's hand without further examination.

Only when we were safely across the frontier did Jimmie divulge his strategy. Modestly, he explained: 'I took a chance and quoted the first stanza of Dante's "Comedia", and, luckily, the frontier official knew the next one.'

By the time we reached Mentone, the last train for Nice had left and, even if Williams and I hired a car, we could hardly disturb Lady Nunburnholme's household at one in the morning. So Jimmie decreed that we should accompany him and Sol, and Jack to the Empress's villa.

Remembering my manners, doubtfully, I said: 'The Empress won't know me from Adam.' To which Jimmie replied: 'She is in bed anyway, so probably she won't see you.'

Which proved true. But, at least, I was near enough to her

(parked in her dressing-room) to fancy I could hear her breathing. And Williams, with her social equilibrium completely restored, slept, in blissful discomfort, on the sofa in the sitting-room of the Lady-in-Waiting.

Chapter Seventeen

LOHENGRIN AND ELSA

SOMETIME DURING the spring of 1920 Rolie's parents decided that we had crossed the borderline from adolescence into maturity and, after nearly two years of waiting and hoping, we became officially engaged, with our wedding planned to take place in the autumn.

We had been 'unofficially' engaged for so long that the formal announcement only seemed a question of sticking on fresh labels. But now we were allowed to dine alone together and to motor down alone to stay with friends, which seemed to me as emancipated as it was delightful.

Rolie gave me a half-hoop ring of a ruby and two diamonds, and a little diamond Coldstream star to pin into my hat. I gave him some 'engagement' cuff-links; we gave each other photographs; and the future seemed but a vista of exchanging presents to confirm our love.

Sometimes, we went to stay with Violet and Denys, now in a rented house in Sussex. Although I still felt as though I were being submitted to some form of kit inspection, now I liked Denys much better, especially when I discovered that he had a sense of the ridiculous very much like mine. And, of course, he and Rolie got on well, as he was a beautiful horseman. As regards his relationship to Violet now he and she seemed 'formally' happy. Although more demonstrative to her than before, I still could not imagine him spontaneously kissing her behind a hedge. Were he so minded, I felt that he would deliberately plan it all beforehand. Rolie found Violet rather alarming at first, until he realized he could tease her.

And sometimes we stayed with Rupert and Vi at Runnymede but, more often, with our own contemporaries. Enid (Dudley-Ward) now married to Allan Adair, had us to stay at Windsor; Marjorie Jessel, with her parents, to Goudhurst; Doris, to Nuneham; and Marjorie Jenkins (now also officially engaged to Brecky) often invited us to her parents' fascinating house bridging the Test, Wherwell Priory, near Andover. Almost at once, we were invited to Melbury and Quidenham but (not really surprisingly), not to Crichel. The pattern of our lives altered very little from what it had been over the past two years except that now, deliciously, we fitted into it as a pair.

Poor Lord Ashcombe was subjected to two Amazonian attacks on my behalf that summer; one, from Mamma, and the other, from Maggie Greville.

Having demanded an interview with Papa (to discuss marriage settlements), Lord Ashcombe arrived to find only Mamma who, from the first, had been light-heartedly determined to play the interview like a poker hand, luring him into bidding very much higher than he had originally intended. Based on the fact that he gave his wife pin money and paid all the household expenses himself, Lord Ashcombe's initial bid had seemed inadequate to Mamma. So, with an innocence of face that seemed to imply two small pairs in her hand, she had asked him: 'If we give Sonia a certain figure will you give Rolie the same?' Apparently, the risk had seemed to him justifiable as (figuratively speaking) he had declared: 'I'll see you!' Whereupon Mamma had put down a full house, beating his straight, to which he had had to 'ante up' the difference. When, still shaken, he had expressed the hope that this (expensive?) marriage would last, grandiloquently Mamma had answered: 'My dear Lord Ashcombe, neither you nor I can legislate for eternity.'

As Lord Lieutenant of Surrey, Lord Ashcombe had had some differences with Maggie and for years neither he nor she had attempted to bridge the intervening two miles between Denbies and Polesden. So, one day, with considerable surprise, he heard that Maggie was in her Rolls-Royce, outside his front door, demanding to speak to him. 'Won't she come in?' he had asked his butler, who had answered: 'No, M'Lord, Madam prefers to wait in the car.'

Mystified, Lord Ashcombe had gone out to behold a chauffeur and footman on the box of the Rolls, and Maggie inside it, formally dressed for the occasion. When he had politely invited her into the house, she had answered: 'No, thank you, I only called to tell you that I do not consider that your son is good enough for my god-daughter.' Then, to his intense irritation, she had driven back to Polesden.

Mamma began to order my trousseau—three dozen night-gowns, petticoats, bodices, chemises, knickers, stockings, hand-kerchiefs, gloves. A dozen pairs of evening and day shoes; six pairs of stays. I had a pink satin peignoir, trimmed with ostrich feathers, for summer; and a quilted blue velvet dressing-gown, with a real Valenciennes lace collar, for winter. (At last Nannie was satisfied.) As, now, I was to be married in November, I had two evening dresses suited to winter: a black velvet square-necked ball dress, and a pink velvet ball dress trimmed with silver lace. (My wedding gown, of silver lamé, was to act as my presentation gown the following summer.) I had two tea-gowns, one trimmed with Chinese embroidery, and the other of billowing chiffon; three day dresses and three afternoon dresses; and three tweed suits and a travelling coat, with matching hats and jerseys and shirts. My going-away dress was of pale blue marocaine, with a skirt cut into petals, topped by a black velvet coat with a grey fox collar, and a grey velvet cap trimmed with ospreys.

The presents began to arrive and, foremost among them, an heirloom from Mamma in the shape of Nannie, bequeathed

to me as a lady's maid. (I felt dreadfully disloyal, but a trifle
dubious, as Rolie's and my combined ages fell short of Nannie's
by nearly thirty years.) Next in importance from Mamma
came a diamond tiara; and an emerald and diamond pendant;
and an enchanting eighteenth century diamond brooch, in the
shape of a sheaf of wheat. And Papa gave me a piano and a
Georgian writing-table; and Violet and Denys gave me two
crystal and diamond hat-pins; and Rolie's parents gave me a
turquoise and diamond pendant; and Rolie himself gave me a
bigger ring and a bigger Coldstream badge. Uncle Arnold and
Aunt Gertie gave me a Georgian sideboard; and Uncle Archie
and Aunt Ida gave me some nineteenth century gilt candle-
sticks. Mamma's friends coughed up nobly: Maggie, with
an emerald ring; the Grand Duke Michael and Countess Torby
with a Fabergé snuff-box; Stavey and Lady Ilchester, with a
huge aquamarine and diamond brooch; Sir Ernest Cassel, with
a fat cheque. (When this arrived, to my disappointment,
Mamma said that cheques were vulgar, so it had to be trans-
formed into a long stole and muff of Canadian sables, which I
did not particularly want.) Marshalled by Marjorie Jessel,
eighty of my girl friends gave me a breakfast, dinner and tea
service in Spode china; nearly all my boy friends gave me
individual presents; and my dentist appositely gave me a tiger's
tooth, attached to a bell. Rolfe and all the house servants gave
me a silver salver, and almost best of all I loved Nannie's two
toast-racks with each strut spelling a letter of 'Rolie' and
'Sonia', in silver plate. And Rolie too had an impressive array,
from his family; from his friends; from his father's tenants,
Every purse within reach seemed to have been opened for us,
to line our future home in the nicest way.

Mamma said: 'Lady Jane Combe has called to ask how you
are, and I said you were better.'
'Oh! yes, much better,' feebly, I croaked.
Outside my window hung a pea-soup fog, seemingly as
thick as a curtain, and, beside my bed, a cylinder of oxygen

tried to clarify the air. Everything possible was being done to relieve my breathing yet, already, I had been in bed with bronchitis for over a week and my wedding was due to take place in another week's time.

Like ballast, various arrangements had been thrown overboard to lighten my load: my 'bachelor girl' party had been cancelled; Mamma's afternoon party, to view the presents, was to take place without me; the photographer, hired to take the wedding group after the ceremony, had been put off. Even the arrangements for my honeymoon had been altered. Now, instead of driving straight to Dover, to spend the night at the Lord Warden Hotel before leaving by boat for the South of France, Rolie and I were to spend our first three days together at Brighton, in Sir Sidney Greville's house (kindly lent us in response to Mamma's SOS). I seemed to be embarking on my married life as anonymously as possible, that is, if I embarked on it at all.

Lying there in bed, I felt a bit depressed and rather frightened. In childhood, I had become almost inured to these attacks, which had all taken place according to a regular formula: sickness, convalescence, regained health. Once I was well again nothing extra had been expected of me. Whereas now, supposing I did not get well as quickly as formerly and dragged along, wheezing dismally behind Rolie's flying feet? Would not he get impatient? Or hurry on without me? Luckily, Nannie would be there, now well-versed in helping me to do my breathing exercises; and in rubbing my chest and back with camphorated oil; and in burning Himrod's (Inhalation) Asthma Cure. But would Rolie resent the continued presence of an old woman of seventy in our bedroom? And (with his broken nose) would he himself be able to weather the pungent vapours of Dr. Himrod's Cure? Might he not just move out of range and leave Nannie and me to it? Really, it was imperative that I should start my married life quite well.

A knock at the door revealed Perriat's smiling face. As usual, immaculately dressed in his white tunic, in his hand

he held his menu book. 'Madame has sent me to ask Mademoiselle what she would like for dinner. Some consommé double?
A cream of chicken?'

My gastric juices began to flow again, and I chose the cream
of chicken. When Perriat had gone, Janet herself came in to
draw my curtains and to make up my fire.

How spoilt I was, I reflected. By everyone in the house
really, except Williams. I only had to ask for anything and I got
it. And without giving anything in return, except to say:
'Thank you.' During this last week each member of the household had seemed to make a special effort to please me. Mamma
and Papa, of course, had filled my room with flowers (sternly
ordered 'out' at night by Doctor Bevan) and Papa had irrepressibly given me the box of Charbonnel & Walker choco-
late-peppermint creams that Mamma had told him not to.
But all the others, too, not in presents, but in various ways,
had spoilt me. (Bessie, usually rather a noisy duster, had dusted
my room on tiptoe; and I felt sure that Perriat's kitchenmaid,
Frances, had thought of the 'pommes soufflées' I had had with
the pheasant yesterday). Dear Rolfe had puffed up and down
the stairs bringing me the weekly illustrated papers and maga-
zines, and giving me news of anyone who had called or telephoned. And both he and Melhuish had brought in the tray
for my meals as though they were serving Queen Mary in
her private apartments. Already Nannie had begun to pack
and, through the open door between her room and mine, I
heard the rustle of tissue-paper. (At the outset, I had had an
anxious moment as she had pronounced my best nightgowns
much too fragile to take on my honeymoon. If I did, she had
said, they would not last. And I had had to get Mamma to
overrule her scruples.) But, now and then, she had taken time
off to amuse me, draping herself in my pink satin peignoir, or
dolling herself up in my going-away hat, as though I was a
sick child again, in the night-nursery at Portman Square. And,
once or twice, Janet had come in to tell me Scotch stories and
to show me photographs of her home in Ross-shire and of

her family. In his or her own way, each member of the household had spoilt me, as though real blood ties held us all together.

Dr. Bevan came in and took my pulse and listened to my
respiration. Anxiously, I asked him: 'Shall I be all right for my
wedding?' As though it were the easiest thing in the world to
put on two thick pairs of combinations under my wedding
gown, he answered: 'I see no reason why not, if you wrap up
well.'

To ensure arriving dry-eyed at the church, I felt my only
hope was to be tough with Mamma and Papa beforehand. I
could brace myself up to meet the actual ceremony, but I knew
that I would break down completely if Mamma or Papa made
any emotional demands on me. Papa was the most likely to,
and I could not risk it. So I decided to write them two little
notes, explaining how much I loved them really, but which I
would ask Rolfe to hold back for delivery until the following
day.

I was hard put to it to stick to my resolution. Never had
Mamma and Papa been more sweet and their every word told
me what I already knew, that their main object in life had
always been to promote the happiness of their children, at
whatever cost to themselves. Again and again they assailed
my crumpling armour, wistfully trying to find a weak spot in
it, through which they could get an assurance of my reciprocal
affection. With each assault my armour became more dented
until it was almost worn through.

But, somehow or other, I resisted, with the result that, when
the time came to leave for the Guards' Chapel, Papa and
Mamma were starry-eyed with indignation.

Mamma left first, magnificent in plum velvet and fox furs,
accompanied by Nannie, inevitably wearing a black plumed
hat (like Hagen, in 'Götterdämmerung') but, on this occasion,
sporting a pair of festive, white kid gloves.

Papa and I followed (I, carrying out Dr. Bevan's instructions,
muffled up in shawls, like a child going to a special party) and

once in the Park, again poor Papa tried to pierce my tinplate defences. 'What am I going to do without my Do?' he asked.

'For heaven's sake! Don't start that, Papa!' I answered crossly, whereupon, furiously, he breathed in through his nostrils and spoke no more.

Outside the Chapel my retinue of ten children seemed to be flowing in all directions, and one of them, Hereward Wake, aged two, was crying so dolefully that his nurse hastily withdrew him from my cortège and picked him up. Bereft of one train bearer and with the remaining one frequently treading on my train, on Papa's arm slowly I started up the aisle. I had been able to attend the dress rehearsal the day before and already knew and admired the ikon-like brilliance of the Chapel's interior, with its lining of tattered battle honours. Outwardly calm, but inwardly terribly nervous, I leant on Papa's arm, and, suddenly, I gave it a little squeeze. It was like recharging a battery whose current flowed back into me. In perfect amity again and doubly strengthened, we moved slowly forward together.

There was no organ, and the band of the 3rd Battalion Coldstream Guards was providing the music. They and the red-coated choir of Guardsmen's children broke into the second verse of: 'Oh! Perfect Love.'

Although on my right side it preserved a mainly anonymous identity, the congregation closed round me rather cosily. On my left, familiar faces showed up out of their context, like cards in a shuffled pack. Mrs. Bonner and Mrs. Hill, from Melbury; Allan and Enid Adair; Norman Gwatkin; Mrs. Rolfe; Dick Hermon. Nearer to the front, Lady de Trafford; and Vi and Rupert; Williams; Marjorie and Lady Jessel; Moiselle; Lindy and Cousin Evie; Mr. Angus; Marjorie and Brecky (married the month before). As was to be expected, the Dryads mainly were dressed in camouflage colours and the Amazons in martial reds and blues. Uncle Arnold's profile stood out, like a bronze of Hawkeye (the Last of the Mohicans);

and as Papa and I reached her side, Mamma turned and smiled at me, looking like Hestia, turned Christian, and her smile was a benediction in itself.

By the time Papa and I reached the altar steps, the last verse was finishing, and as Rolie moved into his place beside me, the choir stopped singing. There was a pause while we waited for the Bishop of Guildford (who was to marry us) to come forward and then, surprisingly, the last verse of the hymn started again.

In all, the choir sang it three times (like a music-hall chorus) while Rolie and I anxiously stood there, waiting for someone else to marry us as, obviously, the Bishop was not forthcoming. Then Canon Roland Errington (who was already officiating) gallantly stepped forward and the marriage service proceeded.

His charming voice soothed me as I listened to it. Dreamily, I heard him pronounce the beautiful words setting out the three purposes of marriage . . . 'for the procreation of children . . . for a remedy against sin . . . for the mutual society, help and comfort that the one ought to have of the other . . .' Fervently, I prayed that Rolie and I would be able to achieve all these things. And I listened again as the Canon wound up: 'Therefore if any man can show any just cause or impediment why they may not lawfully be joined together . . .'

Someone began pounding on the main door of the Chapel and a furious voice shouted: 'Let me in! Let me in!' ('Yedermann! Yedermann!') Hastily, a verger complied and, down the aisle, galloping like a small race-horse, came Mrs. Asquith. She whirled into the front pew, beside Mamma, and stood still with her nostrils flaring. Papa turned his head then whispered in my ear: 'It's Margot!'

By this time the calmness of despair had come over me and I braced myself to take Mrs. Asquith's denunciation from behind. When it did not come, quietly Canon Errington concluded: '. . . let him now speak, or else thereafter forever hold his peace.' The congregation held its breath and Mrs. Asquith kept silent. No one was surprised, thereafter, that Rolie's promises were made in a hoarse voice and that mine were inaudible.

Mrs. Asquith insisted on signing the register in the vestry, when Mamma told her of the unexplained default of the Bishop of Guildford. 'Criminal inefficiency!' she exclaimed, 'I'll take it up with the Archbishop of Canterbury.'

Later, even Lord Ashcombe averred that the Bishop was 'jumping his bridges a bit' when he admitted that he had gone, by mistake, to a mothers' meeting.

INDEX

Adair, Allan (later Major-General Sir Allan Adair), 160, 199
Allan and Enid, 205
Admiralty House, Rosyth, 140–3
Albemarle, Dowager Countess of (Grannie 'B'), 25, 27
Albemarle, Countess of (Aunt Gertie), 27, 122–3, 150–4, 161, 201
Albemarle, 3rd Earl of (Lieut.-General George), 122
Albemarle, 8th Earl of (Uncle Arnold), 25, 27, 122–4, 136, 152–3, 161, 186–7, 201, 205
Albert Hall, Royal, 172, 174
Alkmar, 100
Alington, Lady (Fe'o), 19–21, 33–7, 89, 130, 159
Alington, Lord (Humphrey), 19, 21, 29, 33–4, 36–7, 89, 130–1
Ammann, Mr., 191–2
Amsterdam, 100
Angus, Mr., 111, 141, 151, 205
Appley Hall, 162–3
Ascot, 176, 178
Ashcombe, Lady, 182, 183, 185–7, 198, 199, 201
Ashcombe, 3rd Baron, 181, 184, 185–7, 198, 199, 200, 201, 207
Ashley, Edwina (now Countess Mountbatten), 44
Ashley, Mary, 44
Ashley, Mrs. Wilfrid, 40, 41, 44
Asquith, Anthony (Puffin), 144, 145
Asquith, Elizabeth, 144
Asquith, Rt. Hon. Herbert Henry (later 1st Earl of Oxford and Asquith), 119, 144–5
Asquith, Mrs. (Margot, later Countess of Oxford and Asquith), 119, 120, 144–5, 155, 206–7

Bankhead, Tallulah, 159
Banks, Mrs., 36
Barbellion, 164
Barnes, Major-General Sir Reginald, 169–70
Barrow, Miss, 187
Beatty, Admiral Sir David (later 1st Earl Beatty), 142, 151
Benson, Con, 126, 149, 151

Benson, Evie, 125–7, 144, 205
Benson, Guy, 126
Benson, Rex, 126, 164–5
Benson, Robin, 114, 126
Benson, Rosalind (Lindy), 114, 125–7, 148–9, 160, 164, 205
Beresford, Admiral Lord Charles (later Baron Beresford), 33
Berwick and Alba, Duke of (Jimmie d'Albe), 190, 194, 195, 196
Biarritz, 33, 40, 42–46
Birley, Sir Oswald, 108
Blanefield, 46
'Bobsleigh Derby', 191–3
Bonner, Mrs., 36, 38, 205
Boyd, Eddie (Major Edward Boyd, Royal Scots), 151
Boyd, Phyllis, 99–100
Brecknock, Earl of; later 5th Marquess Camden (Brecky), 181, 188–9, 199, 205
Bridger, Mr., 110
Bridget, Aunt (Lady Keppel), 27
Brighton, 202
Buckhurst, 125–6, 133
Buckingham Palace, 127, 165, 176
Bunger, Herr, 68
Burroughs, Stephen, 160, 165
Bury, Viscount (later 9th Earl of Albemarle), 123

Campbell, Archie, 156–7
Canteen for Soldiers, Countess of Limerick's, 128
Casement, Sir Roger, 133
Cassel, Sir Ernest, 22–23, 44–46, 201
Ceylon, 60, 62, 64
Churchill, Lady Randolph, 119
Churchill, Rt. Hon. Sir Winston, 119, 136, 162
Clingendaal House, 92–95, 98–101
Colebrooke, Bridget, 86
Colombo, 57, 59, 63, 74
Combe, Lady Jane, 201
Connemara, 137–8, 158
Coton House, 187–9
Cotton, Miss Polly, 101, 103
Cowans, General Sir John, 119, 150, 172
Crawford, Betty, 148
Crichel, 33–34, 37, 45, 87, 89, 130, 165, 199

Cubitt, Roland (Rolie), 181–3, 185–7, 189, 198–9, 201–2, 206
Cubitt, Tom, 184
Curragh, The, 136
Curzon, Lady Cynthia (Cimmie), 127
Curzon, Dick, 160
Curzon, Francis, 77
Curzon, Mary, Viscountess, 173
Curzon-Howe, Leicester, R.N., 143, 151
Cust, Harry, 99, 101

Dallas-Waters, Major (10th Bn. Royal Fusiliers), 137
Dambatene, 61–62, 184
Davidson, Aunt Theo (Lady Theodora), 25, 123, 125
Dawson, Captain Richard, 77–78, 191
de Brienen, Baroness Margaret (Daisy), 77–79, 92–95, 98–100, 102, 128, 161
de Grün, Count Wilhelm, 164–5
Denbies, 183–4, 200
de Trafford, Lady, 98, 205
de Trafford, Vi, 86, 99, 100, 178–9, 199, 205
Diaghilev's Russian Ballet, 87–89, 127
Dingwall, 50, 57, 111, 141
Dmitri Pavlovitch, Grand Duke, of Russia, 177–8
Dolly, Aunt (Mrs. Kitson), 25
Draper, Miss, 15, 42, 52, 62, 110, 194
Dudley-Ward, Enid, 113, 160, 199
Duff, Lady Juliet, 89
Dumgoyne, 50
Dunfoyne, 50
Duntreath Castle, 33, 46–51, 121–2

East Lancashire Regiment, 135
Edmonstone, Sir Archibald (Uncle Archie), 25, 33, 47–49, 58–62, 138–9, 201
Edmonstone, Charlie, 47, 151
Edmonstone, Eddie, 47, 151
Edmonstone, Lady (Aunt Ida), 47–49, 58, 61–62, 70, 138–9, 201
Edmonstone, Sir William and Lady (Grandfather and Grandmother), 24
Edmonstone, Willie, 47, 139
Edward VII, King (Kingy), 6, 7, 22–23, 45, 51–52, 54, 170
Errington, Canon Roland, 206
Étaples, 107–8, 110, 113
Eugénie, Empress, 195–6
Eva (Mrs. Graham Murray), 58, 61

Fabergé, 23, 33, 201
Fairfax-Ross, Tommy, (Lieut., Rifle Brigade) (T), 171–2
Fitzgerald, Jim, 160

Florence, Aunt (Countess of Cork and Orrery), 25, 49
Foch, Marshal Ferdinand, 162
Ford, Mr., 113, 176
Fox, Charles James, 109
Fox-Pitt, William, 134, 151
Fox-Pitt, Thomas, R.N., 143, 151
Fox-Strangways, John, 36, 108–9
Fox-Strangways, Lady Mary, 36–37, 99, 108–9
Frances, Aunt (Mrs. Duncan), 25, 49
Francis, Prince, of Teck, 22
Frau (Fräulein), 107, 109, 111
Freed, 40

George V, King, 148
Gerrard, Teddie, 159
Gilmour, Jock, 181, 183
Glocker, Frau, 66–67, 72
Glyn, Marian, 175
Gopsall, 33
Gouda, 100
Goudhurst, 199
Gould, Mr., 36
Grafton Galleries, 159
Graham, Uncle (Lord Dunedin), 25
Granby, Marquess of (John), 86
Greenwood, Sadie, 183
Grenfell, William (Billy), 86, 115
Grenfell, Julian, 86, 115, 179
Grenfell twins, 132 (Francis, V.C., and Riversdale), 132
Greville, Lord, 170
Greville, Ronald, 170
Greville, Mrs. Ronald (Maggie), 22–23, 99, 170–2, 188, 199–201
Greville, Sir Sydney, 99, 202
Grosvenor St., 16, 83, 121, 131, 143–4, 149, 160
Guildford, Bishop of, 206–7
Gwatkin, Brig. Sir Norman, 181, 205

Haarlem, 100
Hague, The, 92, 100, 101, 161
Haldane, 1st Viscount, 86, 89, 144
Hamburg, 63
Hamilton, Lady Cynthia, 127
Hamilton, Admiral Sir Frederick (Cousin Freddie), 140
Hamilton, Harry, R.N., 142, 151
Hamilton, 'Jones', 142
Hamilton, 'Sambo', 142
Hamilton, Louis, R.N. (Turtle), 142, 151
Harcourt, Doris, 114, 160, 175, 199
Harcourt, Lady, 99, 159
Harcourt, Sir 'Lulu', 99, 114
Harry, Uncle (Pipon), Major of the Tower of London, 25, 52

Hartop, Sir Charles, Bart. (Topps), 99
Heath, Volly, 95–98, 111
Herbert, Phyllis, 164
Hermon, Richard, 205
Hill, Mrs., 36, 205
Hillsden, Mr., 98–99, 102
Horseshoe Corner, 191–4
Hospital for Limbless Soldiers, Roehampton, 148
House in the Wood, 100
Howe, Earl and Countess, 33
Hoxton, 28
Hyde Park, 28, 40, 59

Ilchester, Countess of, 33, 36, 38, 99, 107–111, 144, 201
Ilchester, 6th Earl of (Stavey), 33, 36–37, 99, 108, 201
Islington, Viscountess, 119

James, Mrs. Arthur, 53, 187–9
Jenkins, Mrs. Edward, 160
Jenkins, Marjorie, 44, 160, 189, 199, 205
Jessel, Lady, 159, 205
Jessel, Marjorie, 113, 148, 160–1, 172, 183–6, 199, 201, 205
Jessie, Aunt (Mrs. E. Winnington-Ingram), 24–26, 49, 62, 65
Jutland, Battle of, 135, 142

Karsavina, 88
Kellog, Shirley, 121
Kemp, Mr., 159–60
Keppel, Anne, 175
Keppel, Arnold, 123
Keppel, Sir Derek (Uncle Derek), 25, 27, 124, 175
Keppel, Edward, 120–3, 125, 134, 146–7, 150–5, 159, 180
Keppel, Lady Elizabeth, 123
Keppel, George (Papa), 3, 4, 6–8, 13–15, 17, 20, 25, 26–27, 29, 34, 48–49, 52–54, 71–72, 76–77, 83, 85, 87, 90, 93, 99–103, 107–8, 111, 116, 118, 120–1, 123–4, 126–7, 129–31, 133–4, 136–7, 139, 144, 146, 142–3, 155, 169–70, 174–5, 179–180, 190–1, 194, 199, 201–2, 204–6
Keppel, Mrs. George (Mamma), 3–8, 11, 13–15, 21–22, 24–34, 38, 40–43, 46, 48–49, 52–54, 57–59, 61–64, 72–79, 83–84, 87, 90–91, 93–94, 97, 99–103, 107–8, 110–11, 113–14, 116, 118–21, 126–7, 129–39, 143–4, 150, 152, 155–7, 159–60, 162, 170–1, 173–6, 179–80, 183, 190–91, 194–5, 199–204, 206–7
Keppel, Admiral of the Fleet Sir Henry, 32
Keppel, Lady Hilda, 25, 124–5

Keppel, Lady Leopoldina (Aunt Lena), 25, 27, 124
Keppel, Rupert, 99, 107, 123, 161, 178–9, 199, 205
Keppel, Violet, 4–5, 9, 11, 32, 38–44, 51–53, 58, 61, 63–66, 69, 70–73, 83, 85–90, 99, 101–3, 108–9, 111–12, 115–117, 119, 127, 134–5, 137–9, 164, 176, 178–80, 194, 198–9, 201
Keppel, Admiral William Augustus (later Viscount Keppel), 123, 125
Keyser, Sister Agnes, 171
King Edward VII's Hospital for Officers, 170–1
Kingston Lacey, 35
Kinloch, Jean, 146, 155–7
Kinloch, Lady, 156–7
Kitchener of Khartoum, 1st Earl, Field-Marshal, 108, 120, 135

Lanvin, Jeanne, 133
Lennox House, 48
Leon, Teddy, 113–4, 134
Leslie, Lady, 119
Lindsay, Norah, 115
Lindsay, Peter, 115
Lindsell, Phyllis, 192–4
Lister, Charles, 86, 99, 115
Lloyd George, David (later 1st Earl Lloyd George of Dwyfor), 169
Loch Lomond, 51
Louie, Aunt (Mrs. Pipon), 25, 133
Lovelace, Countess of, 155
Lowther, Lady, 176–8

Mafeking, 3
Manners, Lady Diana (later Lady Diana Cooper), 86, 99, 100
Mary, Queen, 165, 171, 176
May, Aunt (Lady Dunedin), 25, 48–49
McKenna, Rt. Hon. Reginald, P.C., 162, 176
McKenna, Stephen, 176
McPhail, Johnnie, 143
McPherson's Gymnasium, 40
Melba, Dame Nellie, 180
Melbury, 33, 36–38, 107–10, 182, 185, 199, 205
Mentone, 195–6
Michael, Grand Duke, of Russia, 23, 201
Moiselle, 38–40, 42, 51–53, 58, 61–63, 65–68, 85–86, 107, 109, 111, 114, 117–118, 128–9, 144, 146, 156, 164, 205
Molesworth girls, 70
Mons, 179
Montgomery, Sir Walter, Bart. (Watty), 57–62, 64, 110
Moore, George, 86, 89

Morrell's Toyshop, 30
Mouravieff, Monsieur, 161
Munich, 64–65, 68, 107

Nannie, 8–12, 15, 18, 20, 22, 29, 32–33, 38, 40–44, 46–47, 51–53, 57–63, 65–68, 73–76, 79, 83–85, 87, 91, 102, 108, 110, 117–18, 138, 140–1, 146, 160, 176, 183, 187, 200–4
Neylor-Leyland, Sir Edward, Bart., 191
Nice, 195–6
Nichols, Mr., 40, 51
Nightingale, Florence, 24
Nijinsky, 88–89
Norton, Richard, 156–7
Nunburnholme, Lady, 195–6
Nuneham, 199
Nuwara Eliya, 59, 62

Pakenham, Admiral Sir William, 142, 151
Paul, Prince, of Greece (later King Paul of the Hellenes), 191, 193
Pearith, Jessie, 48
Pearith, Johnnie, 26, 48
Pearith, Lilias, 48
Perriat, 98, 103, 117, 134, 137–8, 150, 180, 202–3
Phillips, Captain Jackie (Grenadier Guards), 160, 181
Polesden Lacey, 170–1, 186, 200
Ponsonby, Sir Frederick (later 1st Baron Sysonby), 99
Ponsonby, Gaspard (later 2nd Baron Sysonby), 99
Ponsonby, Lady, 99
Ponsonby, Loelia (later Duchess of Westminster), 99
Pontresina, 77
Portman Square, 6–7, 17, 19, 20, 33, 53, 84, 203

Quidenham, 120–4, 153–4, 182, 185, 199

Rasputin, 177
Renshaw, Lady Winifred, 155
Reville & Rossiter, 175
Reynolds, Sir Joshua, 123, 182
Rhodes, Cecil, 124
Ripon, Countess of, 89
Rolfe, 9, 11, 15–16, 51, 85–87, 90–91, 96, 98–99, 102, 110, 117–18, 137, 150, 201–4
Rolfe, Mrs., 91, 205
Ronnie (Ronald Graham-Murray), 58, 61
Rotterdam, 100
Rufford Abbey, 32

Russian Hospital for Officers, 161
Rutland, Violet, Duchess of, 98

Sackville, Lady Avice (Avie), 146
Samways, Mr., 37, 110
Santona, Duchess of (Sol), 190, 194, 195, 196
Santona, Duke of (Jack), 190–1, 193, 195
St. Giles, 35
St. Moritz, 76, 190–1, 194
Scheveningen, 100
Shaftesbury, Countess of, 36
Simonds, Sir John, 172
Skindles, 178
Smuts, Field Marshal Rt. Hon. J. C., 172
Smythe-Martin, Hildegarde, 70–71
Somme Offensive, 137
Sophy, Aunt (Mrs. Hope), 25
Stacey, Mrs., 52, 85, 90
Stavordale, Lord (Harry), 36, 108, 109
Stocks, Eric, 160
Stonor, Sir Harry, 99
Strachan, Mr. (The Master), 50, 93–95
Strachan, Mrs., 50–51
Stuart-Wortley, Bettine, 127
Sturt, Diana, 20–21, 89
Sturt, Gerard, 20–21, 89, 130–1, 165
Sturt, Loïs, 20–21, 33–35, 40, 89–90, 130, 159
Sturt, Napier, 20–21, 89, 159
Sutton Courtenay, 115
Sutton, Sir Richard, Bart. (Dick), 99
Sweeby, 26
Switzerland, 76

Tagart, Lady (Aunt Mary), 25, 124
Tearle, Godfrey, 114
Ted, Uncle (Edward Winnington-Ingram), 25
Tennant, Edward (Bim), 119, 127
Tennant, Clare, 127
Thompson, Mrs. Julie, 131
Torby Countess, 22–23, 201
Torby, Countess Zia, 86
Townley, Lady Susan (Aunt Susan), 25, 161
Townley, Sir Walter (Uncle Walter), 161
Trefusis, Major Denys, 178–80, 194, 198, 201

Van Keppel, Count Arnold Joost, 93
Vane-Tempest, Lord Herbert, 32
Verdun, 135
Victoria, Queen, 6–7
Victory Charity Ball, 172
Villa Eugénie, 44
Vlora Cup, 192–4

Vlora, Prince and Princess, of Rumania, 191

Wake, Hereward, 205
Wallis, Bertram, 121
Went, 187–8
Whatmore, Mrs., 20
Wherwell Priory, 199
White, Colonel Robert, 108, 133, 137
White Farm, 35
Williams, Miss, 117, 138, 194–7, 203, 205
Williamson, Elizabeth, 163–4
Williamson, Lady Elizabeth, 87, 163
Williamson, Sir Hedworth, Bart., 27, 87, 162–3
Wilson, Lady Sarah, 22, 24, 107–8

Wilton Crescent, 7
Wilton Street, 26, 65
Wimborne, Viscount, 158
Windsor, 199
Wodehouse, Philip, 99
Wolff, Miss, 39, 113–14, 136
Wordsworth, Mrs., 40, 127
Worth, 46, 195
Wright, Mrs., 9, 11, 15, 52
Wright, Roger, 160

Yorke, Philip (later 9th Earl of Hardwicke), 89–90
Ypres, Battle of, 152
Yussupoff, Prince, 177

Zoppola, Count, 192